ERLE MONTAIGUE

DIM-MAK

Death-Point Striking

Paladin Press
Boulder, Colorado

Also by Erle Montaigue:

Advanced Dim-Mak:

   The Finer Points of Death-Point Striking

Dim-Mak: Death-Point Striking
by Erle Montaigue

Copyright © 1993 by Erle Montaigue

ISBN 0-87364-718-1
Printed in the United States of America

Published by Paladin Press, a division of
Paladin Enterprises, Inc., P.O. Box 1307,
Boulder, Colorado 80306, USA.
(303) 443-7250

Direct inquiries and/or orders to the above address.

Contents

Warning

The techniques and drills depicted in this book are extremely dangerous. It is not the intent of the author or publisher to encourage readers to attempt any of these techniques and drills without proper professional supervision and training. Attempting to do so can result in severe injury or death. Do not attempt any of these techniques or drills without the supervision of a certified instructor.

The author and publisher disclaim any liability from any damage or injuries of any type that a reader or user of information contained within this book may encounter from the use of said information. *This book is for information purposes only.*

Acknowledgments

Thanks to Karen Pochert for her unswerving efforts to pound this most difficult manuscript into a readable book.

Foreword

It is an honor to write a foreword for a man of such caliber as Master Erle Montaigue.

After training for an introductory period of two decades, I have found few people who understand the principle and demonstrate with perfect clarity the essence of the martial arts; the author belongs to that rare breed.

I have invested both time and money in countless books and other forms of information in order to deepen my own understanding. This book, more than any other, provides a systematic, genuine pathway toward demystifying the mystical, without losing the flavor of the Orient.

Anyone with a real passion, and not just a passing fancy, for the martial arts, will inevitably read about the supposed great benefits and martial prowess attributed to t'ai chi ch'uan (hao ch'uan), or loose boxing, as it was originally called.

Many people cite marvelous feats of past masters, and one inevitably asks, "Is this fact or fiction?"

I do not believe in fairy tales; however, I do agree that we can aspire to and achieve the level of past masters. They possessed a knowledge and wisdom founded in nature and based on their experience and interaction with it.

Even with natural ability and hard work, achieving a high level of competence is not guaranteed without correct information and teaching.

Erle Montaigue informally guides us along the correct road armed with the "good oil" acquired from his direct lineage, traceable back to the great Yang Lu-ch'an, the founder of the real Yang style.

This book states clearly the methods that are hidden in the t'ai chi classics. Dim-mak is the major ingredient, along with fa-jing, that warrants calling t'ai chi ch'uan the "supreme ultimate" and, moreover, *the deadliest martial art ever invented.*

Dim-mak can be extremely dangerous, especially when coupled with the immaturity of egotistical showmen who bear no resemblance to credible martial artists. It becomes a gun in a child's hands; it is not so much the gun that is potentially lethal, but the immaturity of the child that makes it so dangerous.

By studying the concepts of the internal arts (and the external arts at a mature level), we are able to elevate the effectiveness of our art so that both the art and the person evolve, becoming "deadly with dignity." This is far removed from irresponsibly striking a few acupuncture points. By contrast, you need to be skilled as a result of investing hard work, or as the Chinese say, "kung-fu."

T'ai chi is a shield against ill health and disease; dim-mak also becomes an aid to achieving longevity when used correctly to prevent, or reverse the effect of, imbalance in the body. With correct teaching, we do not need to rely upon brute strength and speed to acquire success. Smaller people regain confidence, and larger people do not have to reach middle age before they suddenly realize they did not acquire the real technique but were merely borrowing from youthfulness and strength.

This book will serve as a beacon in the night, along the dark and lonely journey. With Erle as a trusted lighthouse keeper, I am sure a safe passage toward inner peace, effective combat, and robust health are guaranteed.

—Ken Johnson
5th Dan, Tani Ha Shito-ryu Karate
September 1992

Kenny Johnson is a six-time European champion and two-time Open Japan champion in kumite (fighting). He holds 5th dan in the tani ha shito-ryu style of karate. Both Kenny and his teacher and friend Sensei Tomiyama (6th dan and leader of the style in Europe) travel to Australia to give workshops themselves and also to train with Erle Montaigue in dim-mak and taiji. Kenny now lives and teaches in Norway.

Preface

T'ai chi ch'uan is a relatively modern phrase. It came about in the late nineteenth century. Before that, what we now know as t'ai chi was called by other names, such as "hao ch'uan (translated "loose boxing") or its more correct name of "dim-mak" (translated "the striking of the vital points" or "death-point striking.")

Nowadays, I avoid even using the name t'ai chi, as this tends to scare off the serious martial artist who has always looked upon this martial art as a dance or a way of gaining good health. However, the tide is changing, and we are now seeing very highly ranked karateka either borrowing what they want from this most deadly fighting art and using it as an adjunct to their own, taking up the art wholeheartedly while still keeping their original style, or eventually leaving their own art completely.

The reason is that now people are beginning to realize that t'ai chi ch'uan is called "supreme ultimate boxing" because it is just that—the most deadly fighting art ever invented. So how has this deadly art become so abused and derided by many martial artists over the past forty or so years? Because most t'ai chi instructors either don't know or do not wish to show the real applications because they are just too dangerous. However, today there is a real sense of education, and now is the time to tell people the full story, mainly so they will not go and try out these deadly techniques just to see what will happen; hence this book and my dim-mak series of videos.

Some authors of other books on "nerve strikes" and the knock-out syndrome have said that because arts such as dim-mak were founded long ago, today we have more knowledge than they did back then. People who write such trite don't know what they are talking about. We are talking dim-mak here—acupuncture points, neurological shutdown, and so on, about which modern doctors know nothing. The people who invented dim-mak used to try it out on real people. We cannot do this, or we would end up in *gaol* (jail) for murder. They knew alright, but they weren't telling, except to their immediate family and a handful of honored students.

THE SUPREME ULTIMATE?

Many martial artists tend to deride t'ai chi respectfully because of its delicate nature with regard to performance and slow movements and such. Many t'ai chi people tend to fall back on the classics and quote untranslatable Chinese sayings as being indicative of what this "supreme ultimate" martial art is all about. Many come well equipped with a bunch of old classical sayings that sound great when rolled off the tongue at parties and other social gatherings, but when it comes to actual translating them into "use," all of the classical sayings in the world won't help.

When I give workshops I usually begin with a couple of phrases which, to many of the harder-style martial artists who attend, sound quite absurd— until they see and hear what I have to say and begin to understand why I have made these statements.

One such statement is, "T'ai chi is the most deadly fighting art ever invented!" In response to this I always hear a few low chuckles and some nervous shuffling of feet. After about one hour of workshop, these people are usually converted to the internal, and they too believe that t'ai chi *is* the supreme ultimate. Why? Let me tell you a story.

Once upon a time (around 1300, as Chang was born in 1270) there was a man called Chang Sang-feng. Chang, a famous acupuncturist, was fascinated with the martial arts and was already good at the harder Shaolin styles. In his quest to find the ultimate fighting art, one that could render a man immobile with only a medium to light strike to certain parts of the human body, Chang, we are told, "worked upon" animals and, according to some, even a few people.

After Chang was finished and was certain that he had invented the most devastating fighting art ever, he set about to invent a form or set of movements so that his kin, or preferred students, could learn these deadly techniques without actually having to kill people. Then it occurred to him that others, more nefarious than he, might get ahold of the art and use it for evil or against him! So he set about to invent a form which was only an abstract way of learning the real techniques.

This form was of a martial nature (i.e., block, punch, lock, kick, etc.), but it was nowhere near as deadly as the internal hidden meaning. Chang's original art was called dim-mak, or death touch, and the art he invented to cover up its hidden meanings would eventually be called t'ai chi ch'uan.

Over the years, however, most people have only been taught the physical or false meanings of the t'ai chi form, so that all we see now is quite an inadequate form of fighting art in the eyes of other martial artists.

Another phrase I use to cause some concern amongst t'ai chi practitioners who attend my workshops is, "There are no pushes in t'ai chi."

"How can this be," they ask in horror, "when the whole of the t'ai chi repertoire is based upon pushing?"

I ask, "Why push? What does that do? Nothing—he just gets up and reattacks, unless you have pushed him into the path of an oncoming bus!"

If t'ai chi is the supreme ultimate, why push? No, there *are* no pushes in t'ai chi; they are all strikes to certain acupuncture points, and the mere execution of the form demonstrates the correct direction and manner in which we have to strike in order to do this damage. For instance, a man can be rendered unconscious with a screwing strike to the right or left pectoral, to points known as "Stomach 15 and 16." Now, if we are to strike at both pectoral points at the same time, then death is not far away. Isn't that indicative of the posture from the t'ai chi form commonly known as "push"?

Actually, the exact translation for the Chinese character translated from the original taiji texts as "push" is incorrect. If you look at that character, it really translates as "press" and not "push," and there we have a clue to the real application of the posture. The original translators probably thought we would not understand "press," so they changed it to "push." Then they gave the name "press" to another posture in the taiji form or kata which really translated as "squeeze," thinking we would not understand "squeeze."

There have been many mistranslations given to

Figure 1

Figure 2

us in this way. This strike, when used only lightly at seminars, will change any martial artist's ideas about t'ai chi and how effective it is.

Take the posture known as "double p'eng" (fig. 1)—you know, that seemingly useless posture just before the roll-back posture and just after p'eng? The true meaning behind this posture is actually a strike to a delayed or immediate death point called "Stomach 9" (fig. 2). (It is *both* delayed and immediate because it can cause death either immediately or up to seven years later. Depending upon how it is struck, it can cause the slow disintegration of the carotid artery over a period of up to seven years, eventually resulting in a stroke.) This point is lateral to the thyroid cartilage and just under the sternocleidomastoid muscle running along the outside of the neck. Just inside the internal carotid artery, right after it branches out from the common carotid artery, there is a baroreceptor called the carotid sinus, a small baroreceptor (barometer, or receiver of messages) which lies in the internal carotid artery just where it branches out from the common carotid artery. (The common carotid artery branches out into the external and internal branches, which feed different areas of the head and face with blood.) This sinus lies at the top margin of the thyroid cartilage (Adam's apple) and just under the sternocleidomastoid (the big muscle running up either side of your neck). It is responsible for governing the level of blood pressure in the body. When it is struck (fig. 3)—even lightly, as is done occasionally in medical practice to lower the blood pressure—it causes the mind to think that extreme high blood pressure is present and so lower the blood pressure immediately.

Now, if high blood pressure does not actually exist, then there is a shortage of blood flowing to the brain, and so the body just blacks out so that it will become lateral, allowing more blood to travel to the brain.

This is the first application of this posture. The second involves even more sinister practice. Think of when you roll your palms over to begin the pull down (fig. 4). Even this has a hidden meaning. As the palms are turned over, the left fingers again squeeze the Stomach 9 (St 9) point to cause fur-

Figure 3

Figure 4

Figure 5

ther lowering of the pressure while the right palm attacks the gall bladder point shown in Figure 5 known as Gall Bladder 14 (Gb 14), just above the eyebrows.

Why? We are told by medical science that there are three other organs in the body that, when attacked or in great pain, will also cause a lowering of the blood pressure and, as a result, knockout: the gall bladder, the intestines, and the urethra. As any acupuncturist knows, the gall bladder meridian and the intestines virtually run all over the human body, from head to toe. So we now have hundreds of striking points which, in effect, cause the brain to think either the gall bladder or the intestines have been struck.

Every tiny movement in t'ai chi means something. For instance, I mentioned earlier that some points can be attacked directly while others need to be set up with other strikes, as with the "play guitar" posture. In this case you will notice any old master or person who is adept at the internal meaning of t'ai chi actually push and pull his right and left palms respectively. Why? This is to upset the whole energy system of the body by rubbing the flows back the opposite way on both sides of the forearm. This, in turn, will leave the knee joint vulnerable—more so than usual—to the more potent kick inherent in this posture.

What about that seemingly silly posture called "punch to knee"? Have you ever tried to punch someone's knee? No, this posture actually takes the attacker's wrist, squeezing it to cause all of the bodily energy to go to the wrist, and then the right fist attacks to a point on the upper arm called Triple Warmer 12 (Tw 12).

I had a karate teacher attend one of my seminars, and he was punched accidentally on a point called neigwan (translated "inner gate"), just on the inside of the inner wrist, which is a pericardium point. It was not a heavy blow, though it was not a light one either, but the chap turned slightly green and had to sit down for a few minutes.

No matter how insignificant the movement in your t'ai chi form, there is a reason for it. And that reason was worked out by men of genius many hundreds of years ago. Now we are spreading the good word that tells us that t'ai chi ch'uan does deserve its name of distinction, and all of us can be proud that we are indeed studying the supreme ultimate fighting art.

When most people talk about dim-mak, they immediately get onto the old "times of the day" strikes. This sounds quite mystical and secretive, but when looked at logically, this type of dim-mak contains some glaring errors. One would have to know what time it was in order to use it, for instance! Furthermore, many of the points that are "active" during a certain time are just too difficult to get to.

This is where people have mixed up acupuncture with dim-mak. Acupuncture is not dim-mak, nor is dim-mak acupuncture. They use the same points, but that's as far as it goes. It's true that certain meridians are active at certain times of the day, and the qi flowing through that particular meridian at that time is also very active to cause the associated organ to be active. This is why we want to get up in the morning and go to the toilet—the colon has been active for the past two hours of the early morning. We are even given certain points in certain meridians that are active at certain times, but this is only for the healing art and not for the death art. Dim-mak works no matter what time it is; a small person is capable of knocking a large man out with only medium power to certain points.

THE TIMES OF THE DAY AND THEIR POINTS

These times are only given out of interest. True, striking these points *will* have a slightly greater effect at the exact time given, but not much more than any other time. It's just that the qi is more active at this time. Many people also have the mistaken idea that qi only flows in certain meridians at certain times. For instance, people will say, "The qi is now flowing through the heart meridian." But the qi is *always* flowing; if it stopped, you would die! What they mean is that the qi is active in that meridian and not in others at certain times.

THE FLOW OF QI

When we talk about the daily "flow of qi" throughout the body and where the qi is "flowing"

ORGAN TIMES
(Best times to strike and points
most likely to be hurt at these times)

MERIDIAN	TIME ACTIVE	POINT ACTIVE
Lungs	3 A.M. to 5 A.M.	Lu 8
Large Intestine	5 A.M. to 7 A.M.	Li 1
Stomach	7 A.M. to 9 A.M.	St 36
Spleen	9 A.M. to 11 A.M.	Sp 3
Heart	11 A.M. to 1 P.M.	H 8
Small Intestine	1 P.M. to 3 P.M.	Si 5
Bladder	3 P.M. to 5 P.M.	Bl 66
Kidneys	5 P.M. to 7 P.M.	K 10
Pericardium	7 P.M. to 9 P.M.	Pc 8
Sanjiao (Triple Warmer)	9 P.M. to 11 P.M.	Sj 6
Gall bladder	11 P.M. to 1 A.M.	Gb 41
Liver	1 A.M. to 3 A.M.	Liv 1

at that particular time, we do not mean that there is no flow in the other meridians, as the flow is connected and continuous. So when we say that the qi is flowing through the lungs between 3 A.M. and 5 A.M., we do not mean that the qi is *only* flowing in that meridian, as it *must flow* in all of the meridians at the same time, like the continuous flow of water through a hose. What we mean is that the qi is *active* in that meridian at that particular time.

Acupuncturists work with the "outer meridian qi," which does run down the lung meridian on the inside of the forearm, for instance, and then back up the colon meridian, and so on.

But we in the martial arts are taught that there is an equal and opposite flow of "inner qi" which runs in the opposite direction on the inside of the meridian. If this qi is affected, the outer qi will also be affected and either be restricted severely, meaning sickness; stopped momentarily, meaning death is not far off; or reversed, meaning instant death.

It is what we do to this "inner qi" that causes the normal flow to change.

When we stick a needle into someone using acupuncture, we affect *only* the outer flow of qi, the one that flows down the inside of the arm and up the outside of the arm. By using needles, we are unable to affect the inner flow of energy. This is what acupuncturists do not know. When we use finger pressure, as in dim-mak or dim-mak healing, we affect the inner flow of qi and, ultimately, the outer flow as well. So when we attack a point or need to set up a point, we must know the correct *inner* flow of qi, and not necessarily the outer flow.

This is also where some people have gone wrong is some cases. They took their knowledge of the "direction of the flow" from the acupuncture texts which tell us that the qi flows in a certain direction. But these people are using *finger pressure*, not needles, and so they are, in many cases, pressing the points in the wrong direction!

One of the explanations the "mystic area" of the healing and martial arts provides for the flow direction is that it is dependent upon the meridians being either yin or yang and that the yang meridians must have an up-to-down flow (heaven to earth) while the yin meridians must have a down-to-up flow (earth to heaven). This is the more mystical explanation for the reverse flow, à la acupuncture.

But what if someone holds his arm up? Does the flow reverse because the qi must flow from down to up? No, the qi flows in the same direction all the time and not because of some mystical reason, but because that's the way it flows!

In this book, when I refer to a particular flow of

qi or energy, I will mean the internal flow as used by the dim-mak people, and not the acupuncture flow outside of the meridians.

Introduction

Hereunder is written a very minute part of the history of Chinese boxing; it would take several volumes to tell the whole story. But this will suffice for the history of dim-mak in a large nutshell.

When researching the history of dim-mak, we are continually bumping into taijiquan (t'ai chi ch'uan), and in order to find out the origins of dim-mak, we must also know about the beginnings of taiji, because as we learn more we find out that the two are the same.

Why do you suppose that t'ai chi ch'uan means "the supreme ultimate boxing"? To discover the reason we must go right back to when dim-mak was invented by Chang San-feng around the beginning of the fourteenth century.

Many say that Chang did not have anything to

do with the founding of taiji, while others still celebrate his birthday as the founder of taiji. The reason some say he had nothing to do with it is that there is nothing written either on his grave or in his writings that actually says "taijiquan." But this is silly, because the name taiji was not even invented for the art until the nineteenth century. Before that, taiji was simply called dim-mak or hao ch'uan (loose boxing). Another reason that there is not much in the way of written physical evidence is that Chang's nature made him very secretive and also a little paranoid, so all of the "good oil" was only passed on by word of mouth, and only to direct kin and favored students.

Chang had a couple of buddies who were also top acupuncturists in China, and the three of them set out to find out which points on the human body could cause the most damage when struck in certain ways. They discovered that striking specific points in a certain way and direction would cause the optimum damage. They then discovered that energy flows throughout the human body could either be "touched" in the direction of the qi for healing or in the adverse direction to cause damage. (I say "touched," but this can mean quite a substantial strike.) Certain points had to be struck with either a counterclockwise screwing motion or vice versa to cause the most damage for the least possible usage of energy.

During their research, Chang San-feng and his buddies also discovered that striking some points would make other points, joints, and so on much more vulnerable to a lighter strike, while striking others directly would have a dire effect. But still, they were not sure they had the best and most deadly fighting system in China. So they set about to find out which points on the human body would cause which reactions. They knew performing acupuncture on certain points would either cause damage or heal. Word has it that they bribed the jailers to give them the "baddies" to test out their theories! Without going into exactly how they worked on the points, some years and many corpses later they finally worked out exactly which points did what and in which combinations, as well as the correct directions and amounts of force with which to strike at these points in order to either cause death or immobilize an opponent.

Again, Chang was quite paranoid; he did not want anyone other than his own to have his discoveries, and he was afraid that others might use his art against him. It must be remembered here that back in those days of feudal China, people had to rely upon their hands and hand-held weapons to defend themselves and their families. It was so dangerous living in those times that the woman of the family never knew if Dad was coming home that evening, and Dad never knew if his family would be waiting for him when he arrived home. Nowadays, these arts are not so important to us—apart from the interest and aesthetic values they impart—because of guns, but back the, your art had to be good, otherwise you would die.

So Chang had to have a way to teach his art to his family and students without letting anyone else find out what it was he was practicing. The resulting form of movement, which was really a front for a hidden set of movements, eventually became known as t'ai chi ch'uan. But by the time people began calling it this, not many knew why they were doing these movements! The original meaning was lost, and only the family members had the good oil. Right up to our present day, this knowledge has only been passed down to a few instructors.

The above puts pay to the idea put forward by

some that modern masters of dim-mak have more information than those who invented the art because of modern scientific methods. How can the modern masters have more information, when the ancients actually killed people so that their students would have the information on which points worked, which ones didn't, the correct directions in which to strike, and how much pressure to use, as well as which points work in the best combinations? Western medicine, in large part, is only now discovering what the ancient Chinese have known for centuries.

Chang passed his deadly art down through his family members and favored students. One of these was Wang Tsung-yeuh, who actually wrote it all down and passed it on to his students. One of these was called Zhiang. Zhiang lived at the same time that Yang Lu-ch'an lived. From here on in, it gets a little complicated; in fact, I think the scriptwriters of "Dynasty" must have known about the history of dim-mak!

Some may know Yang Lu-ch'an as the founder of the most famous style of taiji, the Yang style. Yang's history is quite amazing in itself. But, in a nutshell the size of a small car, Yang decided he liked what a family of Shaolin people called the Chens had to offer and inveigled his way into the Chen village after many attempts. The story goes that Yang lay down in the snow outside the village until the elders decided that he should be admitted. Yang is said to have learned the whole system from peeping through a door hole! Silly, huh? While Yang was at the Chen village, it is said that Zhiang also came through and was admitted because of his advanced fighting skills. Because Zhiang and Yang were both outsiders, Zhiang taught Yang secretly until there was no more he could teach him.

The Chens took what they could and added it

to their hard style, and this is where Chen-style taiji comes from today. Many modern-day masters even go so far as to say that Chen style is not even taiji, and they quote from old records of meetings that were held between all of the old masters of taiji at the time, to which none of the Chen clan was invited.

Anyway, Yang left the Chen village to get married and have his own family. He also studied the treatise by Wang Tsung-yeuh given to him by Zhiang and then formed his own style, which he called Yang's boxing, later to become Yang-style taiji. Yang knew all of the dim-mak and perfected it, even incorporating it into his hand-held weapons, so much so that he and his six sons and two daughters became known as the "invincible Yangs." (Not many slow forms here!) Many other clans hated the Yangs because of their ability and wealth, so they plotted against them, one day succeeding to ambush the seven males of the family. In what was one of the bloodiest battles, Lu-ch'an, not wishing to be taken by his enemies, committed suicide, while four of the sons were killed.

Two of the sons, Yang Ban-hou and Yang Kin-hou, escaped, with Ban-hou going slightly mad and Kin-hou finding a Buddhist monastery to lick his wounds. And this is where modern day Yang-style taiji comes from—mainly Yang Kin-hou, who begat Yang Cheng-fu, and the rest is history.

From Yang Cheng-fu onward, however, the story of taiji changes. No more do we have real internal fighting methods; no more do we see the hidden meanings of the forms in their dim-mak shape. The art became watered down, being derided by many of the Japanese styles as being only suitable for women and older people.

So, what happened?

In the early part of this century, there was a

meeting held between all of the known masters of real taiji of the day. At that meeting, something extraordinary took place that would change the style of the most deadly fighting art forever—to its exact opposite!

They'd had enough; many "outsiders" were beginning to glean a little of the hidden and secret knowledge originally invented by Chang San-feng, so they made up an elaborate plan to keep the outsiders from gaining any more of their knowledge. The fighting art of dim-mak (taiji) *is* an internal system, but nowadays, when asked to demonstrate this internality, no one seems able to. They still use "yield and stick to and not let go" as principles to demonstrate taiji. But this is always at a purely physical level, and this is what the ancients wanted us to believe taiji (dim-mak) was all about.

At the meeting they decided to show us an easier way to do this deadly art, a purely physical way, so that when we performed the so-called true meanings of the postures, we performed purely physical movements. What they did not count on, however, was the fact that everyone, including the Chinese themselves, would eventually take to this way of doing things, like the proverbial ducks to water, so much so that today only a handful of instructors still know about the real meaning of taiji and its applications. They decided they would actually teach us the very basics and put those forward as being representative of the whole system. Instructors were asked not to teach the real system to any outsiders and to only teach the real thing to their immediate kin or one or two favored students.

Most of the masters at this meeting agreed to this and went away happily teaching everyone the wrong thing (or rather, not actually the wrong thing, but only basics). They even left out the harder aspects of the art so that we would only be left with a health art. Some, like Yang Shou-hou, the brother of Yang Cheng-fu, did not agree with this ruling but still would not go against his peers. So Yang Shou-hou decided he would only teach the real thing to a handful of students (only two that I know of). The two that I know of were Hsiung Yang-ho and my main teacher, Chang Yiu-chun, a classmate of Hsiung.

Chang Yiu-chun was one of my instructors, and Chang knew the dim-mak, or death-point striking, of t'ai chi ch'uan. Combining this with my own knowledge of acupuncture and that of many of the world's leading authorities, I have put together what I believe to be the original points from Chang San-feng.

Every move you make in your t'ai chi form is indicative of a very dangerous dim-mak point strike. No matter how insignificant the move, it means something! We do not have to know the correct direction or pressure, because they are all there in our t'ai chi forms, provided, of course, that we have learned the forms correctly and from a competent teacher. For instance, the posture known as "step back and repulse monkey" must be performed by the attacking palm using a definite downward strike while the other palm comes slightly across the body and down to the hip. This ensures that the direction of the strike is going with the flow of energy, or qi. In this case, the palm on the hip attacks important heart and lung points on the forearm, while the other palm attacks a point called Conceptor Vessel (Cv 17). Sometimes we just move one palm half an inch, but this, too, has a reason: to attack the flow of energy to other parts of the body so that certain limbs will become weakened for a more devastating kick or punch.

Supreme ultimate? Yes, when you know why.

CHAPTER ONE

Point Location

One book on point location stands head and shoulders above all others: *Point Location and Point Dynamics Manual*, by Carole and Cameron Rogers. This is the only book used by the World Taiji Boxing Association.

The points I will be showing in this book are the most dangerous points, made more so by the addition of "set-up" points, multiple point strikes, and neurological shutdown points. Many people ask me why I am giving this information out freely. My reasons are as follows.

In the past, information like this was never revealed to anyone, particularly not at seminars, which anyone could attend. Only the most trusted students who had attained the highest grades were given this information. However, in recent years, we have seen a few individuals who have been giving out *some* of this information—just enough to make it very dangerous.

Moreover, these people have been saying that the strikes they are showing are not dangerous and that anyone can use them. And they use them in demonstration to knock people out, sometimes causing many KOs in a row, and sometimes without even asking about medical history.

Stomach 9 point is the classic KO point, causing the carotid sinus to react by lowering the heart rate, thus lowering the blood pressure dramatically and causing a KO. A knife-edge strike across this point is usually used, as anyone can hit this target using this weapon. I am told by one of the United States' leading cardiologists that there are some people who have a hypersensitive carotid sinus who can even knock themselves out by turning suddenly when wearing a tight necktie! The strike is directed back toward the backbone and in slightly to the throat. This is a very dangerous point and is known both in Chinese medicine and dim-mak as an instant or delayed death touch. It can cause death up to 7 years later from stroke. Of course, these people who demonstrate that they can knock any one out with a medium strike to St 9 only do it to a sitting duck—someone who is just standing there waiting to be struck. They never show actually how to get in there and strike the point in the first place.

It doesn't matter how big or strong a person is; a strike to St 9—even with mild pressure—will knock him out, which is why it is one of the main points we teach to women and smaller people.

In the light of all of this, I decided, albeit against the advice of my seniors, that now is the time to educate people, tell them the full story— the very complicated story—of dim-mak, and, more importantly, tell them how dangerous these points are and that they must never be used in demonstration just to show that they work. So far, this has proved to be one of the most dramatic things I have done, and as a result, people all around the world now know that these points are dangerous and exactly why.

Yet people still say to me, "Surely, someone who is perhaps insane or wants to kill someone will just learn it from your videos and books." I respond by telling them that it is much easier to go out and buy a gun, and much easier to execute. The person who is of unsound mind will not wish to put in the training that is essential to learn dim-mak. It is said in China that it takes three lifetimes to learn dim-mak. That is how difficult it is to master. Sure, anyone can learn all of the points, which will work to a certain degree. But to learn the internal aspects of dim-mak, the highest level, and how to "put in the adverse energy" takes a long time and involves a great deal of internal development.

This is the first time so much information has been given out with regard to dim-mak. It is the most comprehensive book ever written on this subject and is the culmination of 25 years of research and instruction from some of the world's top internal martial arts people.

To cover all of the points would take several volumes, so in this book I will only cover those that are the most dangerous and those that are easiest to get to in the self-defense area.

I will only "locate" the points we deal with in dim-mak. I will give a basic location, as we tend to use larger striking portions and so absolute accuracy is not necessary in many cases. I will also give the exact point location from the *Point Location and Point Dynamics Manual*. There are hundreds more points than those I will demonstrate; however, for practical reasons with regard to self-defense, I will only show and use a small percentage of them. For instance, there are points that will drain qi from the whole body, but I would not tell anyone to use the one on the sole of the foot (Kidney 1) in self-defense, as it is too difficult to get to. Others, such as on the front of the head, I *will* cover, as these are very easy to get to in a fighting situation.

As with my whole fighting method, the strike *must work* in a realistic confrontation and be easy enough for anyone to use, small or large, male or female. And it must work in the easiest way so that we use the least amount of energy to cause the greatest effect. After all, the martial arts are only tools that provide us with a good way to defend ourselves, and if a particular martial art actually hinders our self-defense, then it is not a good martial art.

When people criticize me for not using *all* of the points, I ask them which ones they have in mind, and they tell me some point that is impossible to get to in a real confrontation—easy in the dojo or dawgwan, but impossible in the street. Then I ask them to use this point when I attack, and, of course, it is impossible. People wear shoes in the street; they wear coats and other pieces of clothing/armor, so all of this must be taken into account when talking about dim-mak. This is a way of saving your life in a really serious confrontation, and so it *must work* in that realm and not just in a class as a point of interest.

With this in mind, I will cover only the main points that I teach to my students—the ones that I have found to work. How do I know they work? Okay, here is my secret. I have four sons and now a baby daughter. I have my sons strike me at certain points with varying angles. I never strike my students to find out if it works! This stuff is really dangerous; even a mild KO can cause serious injury later in life, and yes, there *is* such a thing as delayed death touch. This is medically proven, not some mumbo-jumbo mystical garbage.

For instance, the Stomach 9 point is the classic KO point used by many top cardiologists to cause the heart rate to lower so that the blood pressure will drop—but only in an extreme emergency. However, striking this point could cause the internal carotid artery to disintegrate slowly for a period of up to 7 years. So someone could die of a stroke up to 7 years after being struck at this point!

Another medically proven delayed death-touch point is Gall Bladder 18, just above each ear at its highest point. Striking this point will cause a small blood vessel to break inside the skull, filling the skull with blood for more than three days and killing the recipient in that time as a result. So never allow anyone, no matter how highly he is graded, to strike you across the neck—it could kill you!

In the interest of science, to be sure that the points work, I have taken the risk of having my boys try them out on me (just once, to be certain that what I am teaching people works and so they do not have to experiment for themselves). Some of them are so potent that my 9-year-old son is capable of knocking me out with a medium strike to, for instance, "Triple Warmer 23" (Tw 23), just above the outside of each eyebrow, at a downward angle. If my son is able to KO me with his lesser power, you can imagine how dangerous this point is when used by an adult. As soon as you are struck here, you will feel the energy just being drained right out of you and then you will faint!

So, any points that do not work I throw out, and the ones that do work I keep. I will, however, be showing some other points that are used in the dim-mak healing area. These may be difficult to get to in the fighting sense, but they are not used for fighting anyway.

POINT	CHINESE NAME	MEANING
Bladder Points		
Bl 15	xinshu	shu of the heart
Bl 16	dushu	shu of du mai (governor vessel)
Bl 23	shenshu	shu of the kidneys
Bl 24	qihaishu	shu of the sea of energy
Colon Points		
Co 1	shangyang	merchant of yang
Co 2	erjian	second section
Co 4	hegu	joining of the valleys
Co 10	shousanli	arm three miles
Co 12	zhouliao	elbow bone
Conceptor Vessel Points		
Cv 4	guanyuan	gate of origin
Cv 14	jujue	lack of resistance
Cv 17	shangzhong	middle of the chest
Cv 22	tiantu	appearing to disappear
Cv 23	lianguan	active source
Cv 24	chengjiang	containing the fluid
Gall Bladder Points		
Gb 1	tongziliao	bone of the eye
Gb 3	shangguan	guests and hosts
Gb 14	yangbai	white yang
Gb 20	fengchi	wind pond
Gb 21	jiangjing	shoulder well
Gb 22	yuanye	deep liquid
Gb 24	riyue	sun and moon
Gb 28	weidao	meeting path
Gb 31	fengshi	city of wind
Gb 32	femur zhongdu	middle solitude
Gb 41	lingi	lying down to weep
Gb 42	diwuhui	five terrestrial reunions

POINT	CHINESE NAME	MEANING

Governor Vessel Points

Gv 26	renzhong	water drain
Gv 21	qianding	anterior summit

Heart Points

H 1	jiguan	extreme fountain
H 3	shaohai	yellow sea
H 5	tongli	communication with the interior
H 6	yinxi	yin accumulation
H 7	shenmen	doorway to the spirit
H 9	shaochong	small assault

Kidney Points

K 1	yongguan	bubbling spring (well)
K 2	rangu	blazing valley
K 5	shuguan	water source
K 10	yingu	valley of yin

Liver Points

Liv 3	taichong	supreme assault
Liv 13	zhangmen	door of the shelter
Liv 14	qimen	door of the period

Lung Points

Lu 1	zhongfu	central palace
Lu 2	yunmen	cloud door
Lu 3	tianfu	celestial palace
Lu 6	kongzui	supreme hole
Lu 8	jinggu	meridian gutter
Lu 9	taiyuan	supreme abyss

Pericardium Points

Pc 6	neigwan	inner gate
Pc 8	laogong	palace of labor

Small Intestine Points

Si 1	shaoze	lesser marsh
Si 2	qiangu	anterior valley
Si 3	houxi	posterior valley

POINT	CHINESE NAME	MEANING
Si 11	tianzong	celestial principle
Si 16	tainchuang	heavenly window
Si 17	tianrong	celestial form

Spleen Points

Sp 17	shidou	food recipient
Sp 19	xiongxian	chest village
Sp 20	zhourong	encircling glory
Sp 21	dabao	big enveloping

Stomach Points

St 3	juliao	large bone
St 9	renjing	man welcome
St 11	qishe	locus of energy
St 15	wuyi	room screen
St 16	yinchuang	breast window
St 32	femurfutu	prostrate here

Triple Warmer Points

Tw 9	sidu	four gutters
Tw 12	xiaoluo	melting to disappear
Tw 17	yifeng	wind screen
Tw 23	sizhukong	bamboo hollow

THE POINTS AND THEIR
INDIVIDUAL FUNCTIONS

A *cun* is a Chinese measurement used in traditional medicine. It will vary from person to person but is generally about the length from your first knuckle on your index finger to the second knuckle—about an inch. A *fen* is about a tenth of an inch.

All dim-mak points are found in hollows just below a lump or a bump caused by a muscle or bone.

Bladder Points (Diagram 1)

The bladder meridian runs from toe to head and has 67 points.

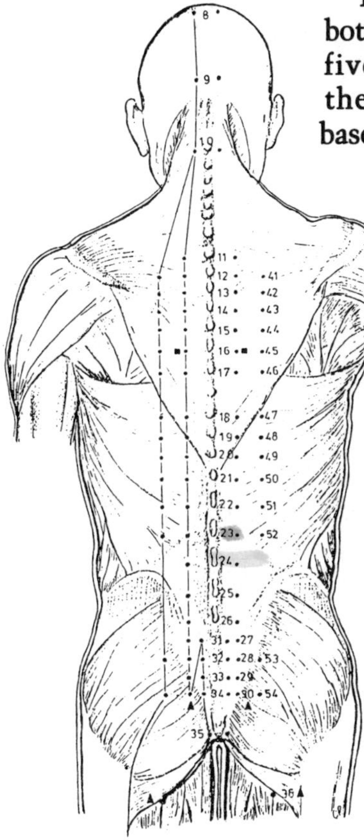

Diagram 1

Bladder 14 and 15 are on both sides of the backbone, five vertebra down from the large vertebra at the base of the neck.

Bl 23 is located 1.5 cun lateral to the backbone on either side of the second lumbar vertebra and is a "kidney shu" point (i.e., it is directly over the kidneys). It is usually attacked with the feet, or sometimes the palms, with a strike that moves in on a straight plane.

Bl 24 is located 1.5 cun lateral to the third lumbar vertebra and is also dangerous because of its proximity to the kidneys.

LARGE INTESTINE

The Colon Points (Diagram 2)

Colon 1 (Co 1) is located at the tip of the index finger on the dorso lateral side (closest to the thumb), 1 fen superior and lateral to the base of the nail. It is usually used as an antidote.

Co 4 is located on the dorsum of the hand in the middle of the second metacarpal, on the lateral side (thumb side) between the thumb and forefinger in that "V" about one cun back. It is usually used as an antidote.

✻ Co 10 is located on the outside of the forearm. If

POINT LOCATION   17

✻ LARGE INTESTINE

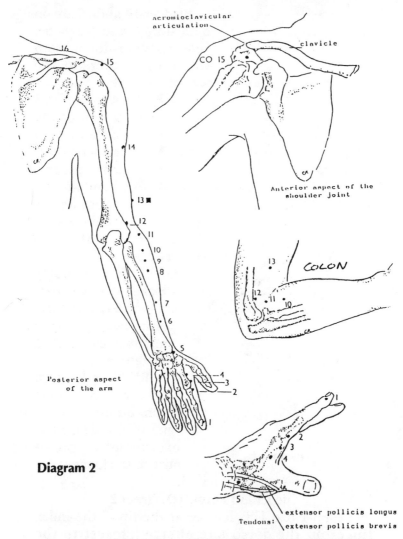

acromioclavicular
articulation

clavicle

CO 15

Anterior aspect of the
shoulder joint

13 ■

COLON

Posterior aspect
of the arm

Diagram 2

Tendons:
extensor pollicis longus
extensor pollicis brevis

you run a straight line from the ring finger to the
elbow, Co 10 is found on that line about 1 cun
back from the elbow crease.

* Co 12 is located in the depression just above the
elbow crease on the outside of the upper arm,
superior to the lateral epicondyle of the humerus.
It is a dangerous point and is usually struck with
the back of the palm in a downward way.

OTHERWISE KNOWN AS THE LARGE INTESTINE
MERIDIAN.

Conceptor Vessel Points (Diagrams 3 and 4)

✳   Conceptor Vessel 4 (Cv 4) is located 3 cun below the navel on the midline. This is where most people say the "tan-tien" is situated, but actually, although it is directly under this point, the tan-tien is on an extra meridian called "jung mei," or life force meridian. The tan-tien is actually Jm 2. But for the sake of expedience, we usually say that Cv 4 is the tan-tien point. This is a very dangerous point, usually kicked up or down to cause death.

✳   Cv 14 is located just over the xiphoid process and 7 cun superior to the navel on the midline. This is an instant death point, as it causes the heart to stop. Ball players have been known to take a ball to the chest right on this point and die on the

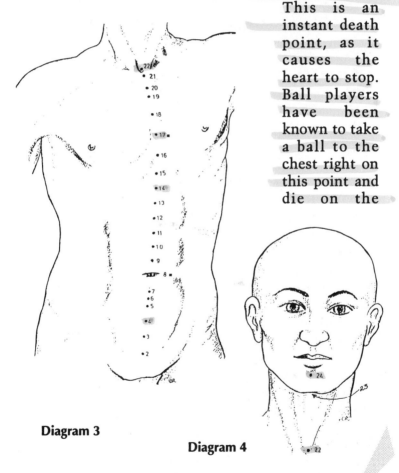

Diagram 3

Diagram 4

*CV–4 & CV–14 CAN BE STRUCK TOGETHER OR IN SEQUENCE FOR INTENSIFIED RESULTS

spot. It is usually struck straight in or upward against the flow of qi. This point is "forbidden" even in acupuncture because it is so dangerous.

Cv 17 is located between the nipples on the midline and is an energy drainage point. Striking this point with the flow, i.e., down, will cause a person to feel as if he has taken the proverbial kick in the guts, as it affects the seat of power, or diaphragm.

Cv 22 is located in the pit of the neck and is very dangerous, as most people know.

Cv 23 is located under the chin where the neck meets the chin.

Cv 24 is just in the hollow where the chin and the bottom lip meet.

Gall Bladder Points (Diagrams 5, 6, and 7)

I will cover this meridian in more detail than the others. The gall bladder points run from head to toe, and any one of them will cause KO as a result of the carotid sinus shutting down the heart. The three

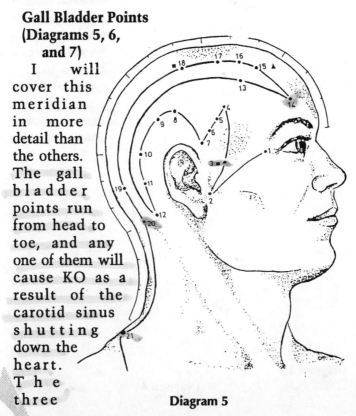

Diagram 5

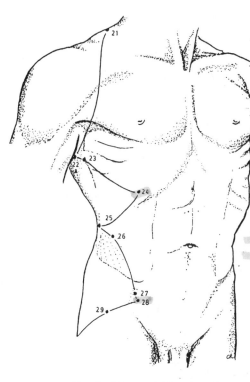

Diagram 6

main organs involved are the intestines, gall bladder, and u-rethra. These points can be struck in up to five different directions and are easily accessible.

Gall Bladder 1 (Gb 1) is located at the corner of the eye and is a very dangerous qi drainage point when struck from rear to front.

Gb 3 is located at the temple and is also very dangerous. It can be struck in a number of ways to cause different things to happen.

Gb 14 is in the middle of the eyebrow and up about 1 cun. This point can be struck in a number of ways to cause either drainage or addition of qi. It too is a KO point.

Gb 20 is located on either side of the back of the skull in the large hollow where the skull meets the neck. This is the classic revival point. We use this point first of all when someone has been knocked out, usually pushing upward, and it works most of the time. In fact, if this does not work, then we resort to CPR.

Gb 21 is that sore spot on either side of the top

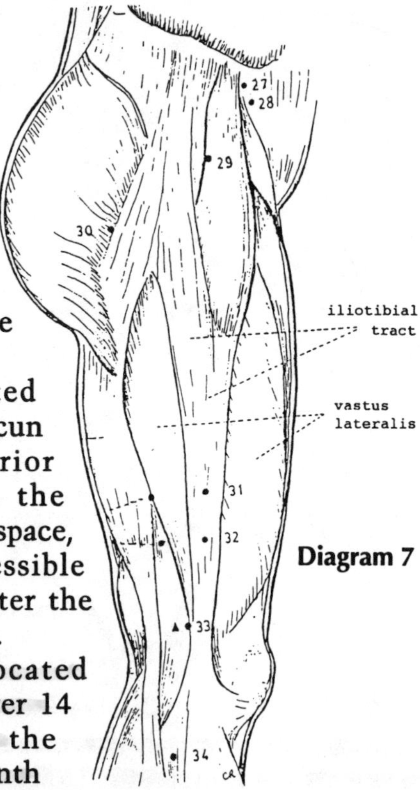

of the shoulders.
We usually press
downward here
and then branch
out to the sides
as an antidote
for being struck
at Gb 14 in an
upward way.
This point will
drain qi from the
head.

Gb 22 is located
under the arm, 3 cun
below the anterior
axillary fold in the
fourth intercostal space,
and is easily accessible
with the elbow after the
arm has been lifted.

* Gb 24 is located
directly below Liver 14
in a line with the
nipple on the seventh
intercostal space and
is an extremely dangerous point.

Gb 28 is located just above the appendix,
approximately, and as it is also over the urethra, it
is a very dangerous point when struck straight in,
which can cause an even worse KO and death.

Gb 31 is located where the longest finger points
to when the arm is just allowed to hang by one's
side on the thigh. Gb 32, 2 cun below that, is
usually used with kicks and is a KO point. This is
the classic "dead leg" point, where someone "for
fun" shoves his knee into the side of your leg
(remember when you used to do it at school?).

Gb 41 and 42 are located on the side of the foot.
Gb 41 is in the depression anterior to the junction

iliotibial
tract

vastus
lateralis

Diagram 7

* GALL BLADDER POINT
STRIKE @ INWARD ANGLE TOWARD
THE SPINE ALONG WITH LV-14.

of the fourth and fifth metatarsals, and 42 is 5 fen anterior to Gb 41, in the cleft between the fourth and fifth metatarsals. These points are easily stomped on to cause KO.

Governor Vessel Points (Diagram 8)

Governor Vessel 21 (Gv 21) is located on top of the head in the middle—a very dangerous point if you can get to it.

Gv 26 is located under the nose and is very dangerous. A light tap here will cause even the largest man to release his hold; harder and it's lights out!

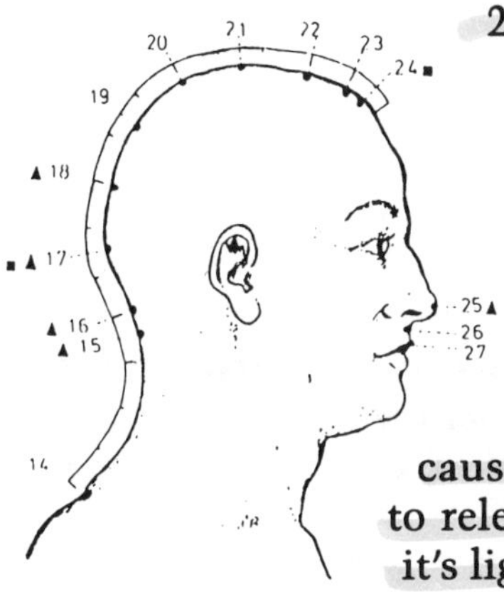

Diagram 8

Heart Points (Diagram 9)

Heart 1 (H 1) is located directly under the arm in the middle of the axilla and is usually struck straight in and up up into the armpit with the radius of either arm. It is a very dangerous point!

H 3 is located in the crease of the elbow and back a tad toward the upper arm on the inside, between the medial end of the transverse cubital crease and the medial epicondyle of the humerus, in a depression. Again, this point is very dangerous when struck away from the body. It is also used as both a drainage point and an antidote point.

H 5 and H 6 are located on the inside of the wrist on the small finger side. H 5 is 1 cun above the wrist crease, toward the elbow, while H 6 is 5 fen (five-tenths, or half, of an inch) above H 7, or the wrist crease.

These are used as antidote points and also as

Heart Main Meridian

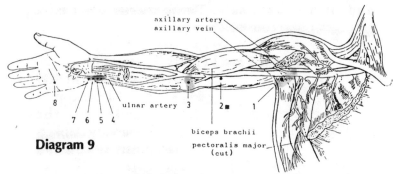

Diagram 9

set-up points and for "negative strikes," as when the wrist is jerked violently away from the body. They are drainage points (i.e., they drain qi from the body, causing weakening) and are usually struck away from the body (i.e., toward the person doing the attacking).

H 7 is located on the wrist crease on the inside of the arm on the small finger side, where there is a small depression. This point, also known as "shenmen" or doorway to the spirit, is usually used in dim-mak healing and is a classic calming point.

H 9 is on the tip of the small finger to the inside of this finger where the fingernail joins. This, too, is used in dim-mak healing and as an antidote when there is heart failure as a result of H 3 being struck.

Kidney Points (Diagram 10)

The only point on the sole of the foot, Kidney 1 (K 1) is used as the classic revival point. It is located in the depression between the second and third metatarso-phalangeal joint (between the mounts of the big toe and second toe).

K 2 is located on the outside of the foot about 1 cun up from the ground and about halfway between the heel and the toes, in a depression on the anterior/medial edge of the foot at the distal and inferior border of the navicular eminence. It is usually used in dim-mak healing.

K 5 is located on the Achilles tendon just above the superior border of the calcaneus, and, in short, squeeze it and it hurts. It is usually used in the healing d i m - m a k

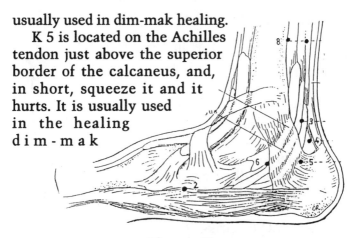

Diagram 10

and as an antidote, but it can be the target of a direct, straight-in dim-mak strike.

K 10 is located pretty well in the middle of the back of the knee. It hurts when pressed. We direct kicks to this point in dim-mak, and it is also used in the healing art.

Liver Points (Diagram 11)

With the knee flexed, Liver 8 (Liv 8) is at the medial end of the popiteal crease in the depression in front of the tendons of the semimembranosus and semitendinosus and behind the medial condyle of the tibia (in other words, on the right knee it's to the left of the knee crease in back and vice versa).

Liv 13 is located at the smallest indentation of the waist, just a little toward the front at the tip of the free end of the eleventh rib. Bagwazhang makes great use of this point, usually striking straight inward causing great internal organ damage, as well as psychological damage. It is a very dangerous point, especially if used with Gb 24.

Liv 14 is just under the nipple where the pectorals make a crease. This is also a very dangerous point when either struck straight in or in a slicing motion (for instance, if you are striking to the right side of the body, striking across the point laterally from right to left), outside to inside. It is usually used with other points, such as Gb 24 or Liv 13. You can cause KO by striking this point with only one palm from no distance.

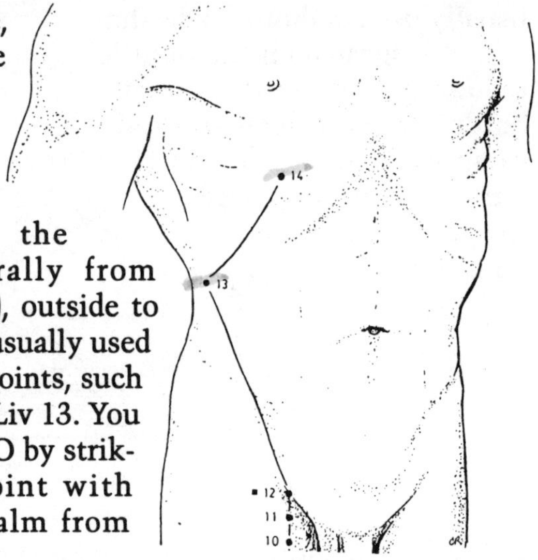

Diagram 11

Lung Points (Diagram 12)

Lung 3 (Lu 3) is located on the lateral side of the biceps brachii muscle, 3 cun below the anterior axillary fold (a little over halfway up the arm on the outside of the biceps). It is used as an antidote to being struck at Liv 14 if emotional disturbances (which can show up weeks later in the form of uncontrollable crying, for instance) are being felt as a result.

Lu 6 is located on the radius side of the forearm on the inside, 7 cun above the wrist flexure on the brachioradialis muscle (a tad over halfway up the forearm). This point is used as an antidote point to reverse the effects of a strike to any of the lung points. We use finger pressure and massage the point back up the arm, toward the person, to revive him. It is also used in conjunction with H 5 to stop bleeding.

Lu 8 and 9 can be used as "set-up points." They are easy to get at and are usually used during small chi-na grabs to the wrist, thus activating the qi to this area and leaving the more dangerous

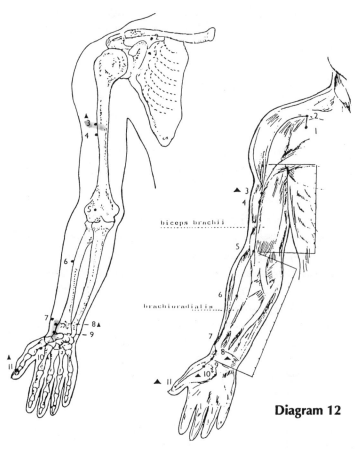

biceps brachii

brachioradialis

Diagram 12

points—such as Stomach 9 or Gall Bladder 14—
more vulnerable to a follow-up strike.

Lu 8 is located on the inside of the wrist, on the
thumb side about 1 cun back above the radial
artery. A straight strike to this point, as in a block,
will affect the lungs. If this point is jerked, not
pulled, toward you, the body will lose energy fast,
hindering a follow-up. It is a classic set-up point.

A word of clarification. You will hear me use the
term "negative strikes" throughout this book. This
term is used for fa-jing reverse strikes, usually to set-up
points. There are no pulls in dim-mak (taijiquan), only
very explosive fa-jing jerks. (I know a few of them!)

Lu 9 is located just below Lu 8 and on the wrist flexure between the radius and the scaphoid. This is also a classic set-up point and is used in the same way Lu 8 is. It is the "meeting point of the pulses" and is quite important in dim-mak. It will cause the respiration to become unbalanced and is a qi drainage point for the lungs. If struck, as in a striking block, it is a classic point for causing the brain to think the whole body has been struck. It is usually struck in a downward way, away from the body on the inside of the arm.

Pericardium Points (Diagram 13)

Located on the inside of the forearm, Pc 6 ✳ (neigwan) is a classic set-up point. About one hand's width back from the wrist crease in the middle of the forearm, this is a very active point and is easy to get at because when people throw punches, we "strike block" this point in either direction to either drain or increase the qi flow. It is also used in wrist locks to weaken the body.

Pc 8 is located on the palm, and if you make a fist, it is where the longest finger points to. This is the point where the qi is said to emanate from when either using healing or dim-mak.

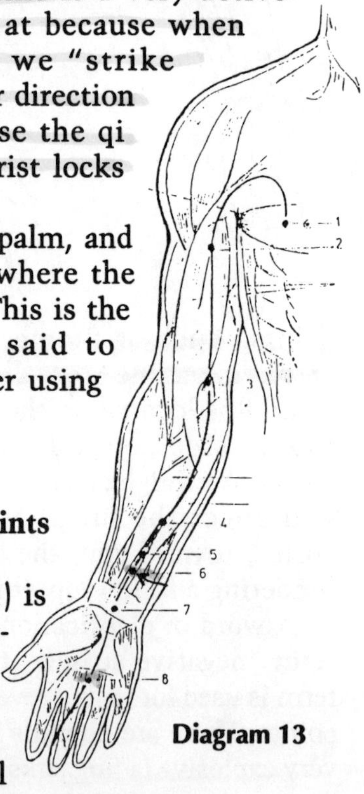

The Small Intestine Points (Diagram 14)

Small Intestine 1 (Si 1) is located on the medial angle of the small fingernail (outside of the finger), 1 fen medial and posterior to the fingernail

Diagram 13

✳ STRIKE TOWARD BODY TO INCREASE CHI, STRIKE AWAY TO DRAIN CHI FROM THE BODY.

base. It is usually used as an antidote and in the healing dim-mak.

Si 11 is located slap-bang in the middle of the scapula and becomes very sore when pressed. It is used to "take out" the arm or cause extreme lower heater damage (i.e., to the part of the body from the navel down—mainly the lower stomach, including the colon and intestines).

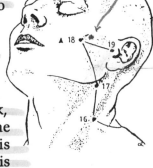

MIND point

Si 16 is located at the center of the base of the neck, at the posterior border of the sternocleidomastoideus. This point is very dangerous and is usually attacked with a straight-in strike.

Diagram 14

Si 17 is located at the angle of the jaw or slightly posterior to it. The carotid artery can be felt here. Si 17 is almost always attacked with a strike that moves from the back of the head forward, which, again, is very dangerous.

Spleen Points (Diagram 15)

Spleen 17 (Sp 17) is located 6 cun lateral to the midline in the fifth intercostal space, lateral to the nipple and down a tad, just past where the pectoral joins the chest. This point is usually struck laterally across the body with an elbow and makes one feel very sick!

Sp 19 is located 6 cun lateral to the midline of the third intercostal space. When struck straight in, Sp 19 also causes strange things to happen to the legs (as with Sp 20).

Sp 20 is located 6 cun lateral to the midline in the second intercostal space, about 1 cun above Sp 19. It is used to weaken the legs.

Sp 21 is located under each arm on the mid-

Diagram 15

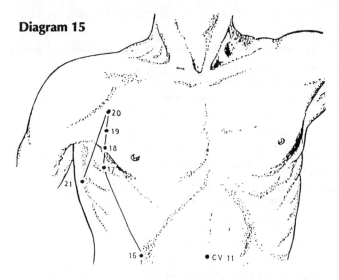

axillary line in the sixth intercostal space. Both Sp 20 and 21 are also used as antidotes.

Stomach Points
(Diagrams 16 and 17)

Stomach 3 (St 3) is located down from the center of each eye in the depression just under the cheekbone. It is struck with the fingers at an upward angle.

The St 11 points are located just above the collar bone notch where it is closest to the neck.

St 15 is located on the pectoral muscles in the second intercostal space, 4 cun lateral to Cv 19. It is used to stop the heart.

St 16 is just under St 15 and a little inward toward the midline on the third intercostal space, 4 cun lateral to

Diagram 16

Diagram 17

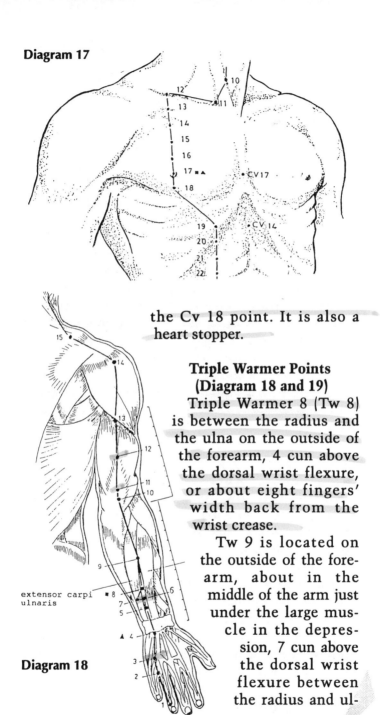

Diagram 18

the Cv 18 point. It is also a heart stopper.

Triple Warmer Points (Diagram 18 and 19)

Triple Warmer 8 (Tw 8) is between the radius and the ulna on the outside of the forearm, 4 cun above the dorsal wrist flexure, or about eight fingers' width back from the wrist crease.

Tw 9 is located on the outside of the forearm, about in the middle of the arm just under the large muscle in the depression, 7 cun above the dorsal wrist flexure between the radius and ul-

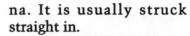

na. It is usually struck straight in.

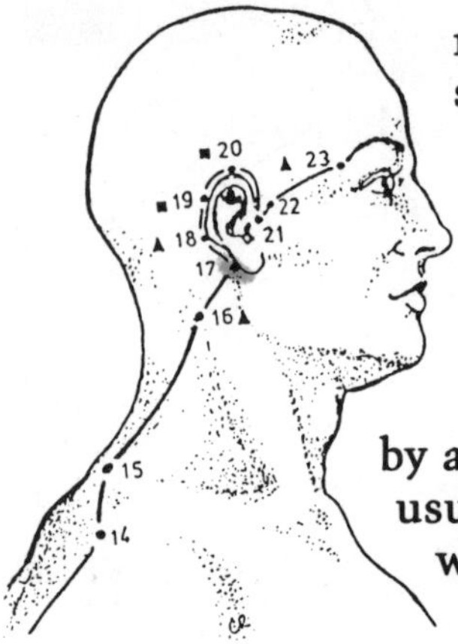

Tw 12 is located in the "horseshoe" formed by the triceps muscle on the outer side of the upper arm. A person can take someone down easily by applying pressure to it. It is usually used in conjunction with Pc 6.

Tw 17 is located behind the ear just below that little hollow. It is an extreme death point with no known antidote, not even CPR. Taiji is one of the only arts that uses strikes to this point in the correct direction, from rear to front using a posture known as "arm left or right." Tw 17 is also used as a controlling point to bring someone who is perhaps under the influence of alcohol under control. Just one finger is all it takes to completely control a person's body using this point.

Diagram 19

* * * * *

Not many points to learn, at least not in comparison to how many there are. I have only shown those that are easy to use. There are others, of course, that will work just as well, but perhaps they are not as easy to get to without years of training.

These are the ones that I *know* will work, and these are the points I teach to my own students.

Don't go out and study your point charts until you know the names of the points by heart—that's useless. Learn them from experience, then you will never lose them. The names are not important; it's knowing subconsciously that if you are in a certain position, fighting with someone, your hand or head or elbow or foot will be in a position to hit something and *will* hit something. Pick one point a day and learn what it does. Fiddle with it on yourself, but be careful. Contrary to what many people say, it *is* possible to KO yourself—I have knocked myself out a couple of times and, apart from the obvious embarrassment, it is not good for you.

CHAPTER TWO

Fa-Jing: The Engine of Dim-Mak

Fa-jing is the engine of dim-mak; without it, we simply do not have real dim-mak. Anyone can stand someone in front of them and use a baseball bat to strike at points. Or the fists or feet can be used, but in order to do this one must be fairly strong physically. This is not real dim-mak. It is easy to KO someone by striking Stomach 9 point on the neck with an inward motion, using only slight pressure. This causes the carotid sinus to activate, stopping the heart for a few seconds and thus causing extreme low blood pressure and KO, but this is not real dim-mak.

In order for those of slight build to use dim-mak to defend themselves, they must know how to use it correctly and make use of *real* dim-mak. To gain this inner function, one must know how to use fa-jing, or explosive energy. This is where we actually put "adverse qi" into the dim-mak points to cause different things to happen with the internal energy flow. It is the fa-jing that causes this adverse energy flow to happen, and so it is called the engine of dim-mak. In this chapter I will show how to gain this power and, more importantly, how to use it.

FA-JING

Fads come and go, but fa-jing has been out there for a long time, and many famous martial artists have utilized it. The old one-inch punch was the flavor of the day back in the seventies and was glorified and mystified. People would study photos of Bruce Lee using mathematical equations and geometrical calculations to try and gain his secrets—especially that of the one-inch punch. All they needed to do was to have someone tell them about fa-jing, which is what all of these people were using to gain such immense power over such short distances.

Most people would study the hands of the exponents, claiming that it was this angle or this direction that caused this supernatural power. Others would call it qi; others would just give up trying. They all missed the boat, though, as it is the *body* that one must watch in order to find out how one gains fa-jing. The attacking peripheral is only secondary to what the body is doing.

There is an old saying—one that not many people use nowadays, as it is not in vogue: "The whole body is a weapon." Everyone who has been around a bit has heard of that saying. It is not in vogue because people simply got the real meaning wrong. We all understand this to mean that the elbow is a weapon, the knee is a weapon, the fists, head, back, shoulders, and so on. But what this saying means is that literally, the whole body is the weapon, while the parts are only secondary and happen as an adjunct to what the body is doing.

Figure 6

This is real fa-jing. The fist does not punch; the whole body punches (fig. 6). The elbow does not strike; the whole body does, and so on. The technique of fa-jing lies in what the body does to cause the peripheral to be thrust out at great speed and power. It is not the strength of the triceps or the laterals that causes the power, but rather the whole body. So it stands to reason that a smaller person is able to generate much more power by using his whole body than a body builder who is only using his triceps to generate the power for the punch. There is simply much more power in a whole body than in one triceps muscle.

If one could utilize the power generated from a sneeze, this would be perfect fa-jing. When we sneeze, the whole body reacts violently, not just one part. We are unable even to keep our eyes open upon the act of sneezing. It is the same with fa-

Figure 7

Figure 8

jing. Upon impact, the eyes are closed for that split second and the body shakes violently at high frequency, throwing out a very deadly fist, palm, or elbow (figs. 7 and 8).

But not only is the whole body used as an initiator of such power for the peripherals, the whole body can be used, physically, as a weapon. For instance, when someone grabs you or is trying to take you down, grapple you, etc., the whole body will perform a fa-jing movement, anywhere. This immense power is enough to cause even the strongest grappler to loosen his grip. However, the beauty of fa-jing is that in order for even the smallest part of the body to do fa-jing, every other portion must also be doing it, otherwise it is not fa-jing and only a muscular strike. And so the grappler would not only find himself being shaken violently, some other peripheral would also be striking to points on his body.

Fa-jing and dim-mak are inseparable. There is dim-mak at a base level, where, for instance, someone is able to strike to Stomach 9, just over the carotid sinus, to cause a knockout (this, by the way, is the classic KO point used by an increasing number of karateka to show how good they are) or use finger strikes to Liver 13 to cause KO and great internal damage. These points can be used by anyone at a base level using pure physical force and not fa-jing. But if one wishes to rise to the highest level of dim-mak, then one must understand real fa-jing.

This is where we use four different body shakes in order to "put in the adverse qi," and not just strike at physical dim-mak points.

Using fa-jing and dim-mak in this way, we are able to systematically cause the opponent's body to react in a known way. We are able to drain energy from the spleen to cause him to simply fall down, still conscious but not able to do anything about it. We are able to add qi to certain points to cause an organ to explode from within. We are even able to cause certain disease states to occur instantaneously by striking certain points. For instance, most know that sunstroke is not nice. It makes us feel really crook (sick) and totally unable to do anything but sit down, let alone fight.

Using dim-mak and fa-jing we can actually cause someone to have a bad case of sunstroke. We also know how to cure this sunstroke using the dim-mak antidote points. In this way, dim-mak and fa-jing are used for healing as well. So we have a death art that is also used to heal people; these points can actually be used to cure a *real* case of sunstroke.

Using certain spleen points on the upper arm and shoulder, we are able to cause someone's right or left leg to shake so violently that he falls down. But striking at these points without fa-jing will only bring about the physical damage caused by the physical power of the strike. This is not fa-jing.

THE "C" BACK

So we learn a few body shakes and think that we know all about fa-jing. No, then we have to learn all about the "C" back (fig. 9) and the rising qi. Look at Bruce Lee when he was fighting. What do you see? Most people look at the physical movements and try to emulate what he was doing. Not many look at what was in his eyes or what the whole of his body was doing. In his own way, Bruce Lee was making use of a primordial posture called "C" back, which allowed him to make use of the part of the human brain known as the "reptilian brain."

Science tells us that we do not have only one brain, but three. There is our normal human brain, which we use 90 percent of the time, and there are the "reptilian" and the "old mammalian" brains. The oldest of these is the reptilian brain, and we can use certain body postures to bring out the

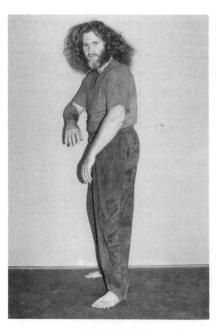

Figure 9

fighting energy of that brain and utilize it. Animals such as snakes, crocodiles, and such which have this type of brain do not see features with their eyes as we do. For instance, I am able to look at a person and make out whether I know that person, making use of the higher intelligence of my human brain. A reptile will just see a shape—a blur. If that blur comes within danger range, the reptile will either run or attack.

When we, as humans, make use of the reptilian brain, the survival part, we become like the reptile or wild animal. We see with eagle vision, or "middle peripheral vision." We make out "things" around us and see that they are moving, and we see them as threats. We are in a survival mode, and every movement annoys us. We are ready to survive. When the threat comes within danger range and in range of our strike, we attack. We do not think to ourselves, "I am going to attack when he gets within such and such a distance" or "I will use this type of attack when he gets close enough." Rather, we allow our reptilian brain to take over, and the body simply reacts when the time is right. We become the wild animal.

"C" back? Look at the great silver-back (gorilla), and notice what his back is doing naturally. It is not an "S" shape like ours, but rather makes a "C" shape. The gorilla, although a placid animal, is also one of the greatest fighters of the animal world where protection of his family is concerned. His "C" back puts him in a constant state of readiness. The qi is constantly ready to defend and attack. The eyes tell the story. When we cause our body to be in this state, the eyes change and we are ready to defend. It was the same way with Bruce Lee. He would go into that little stance of his alone, and so bring up the fighting qi. This is the difference between a martial artist and one who knows how to fight.

The "C" back and the reptilian brain, etc., are concepts taken from Western science. So where does all of this fit in with the ancient Chinese martial artists? Our current scientific knowledge about the human body is all there in the Chinese classics written hundreds of years ago. The taiji classics state that we must round the shoulders and hollow the chest—"C" back! They also state that we must see with the eye of the eagle, using the middle peripheral vision or "eagle vision." When we go into the "C" back posture, the whole attitude changes and we are ready to fight. The arms, legs, back, chest, feet, and head, are all energized, ready for action and release of energy. Couple this with fa-jing and we have the classic animal way of self-defense: simply put, hit him with as much power and speed as possible before he has even attacked. This is stated in the Chinese classic maxim, "If he attacks you, attack him first."

THE TYPES OF FA-JING

There are four kinds of fa-jing, all generated from the whole body but having different ways to generate the power. The most common is the "closed shaking fa-jing." This is where we are using the natural stance and punching with the same fist as the foot that is

Figure 10

forward (fig. 10). The body shakes violently from left to right (if using a right fist) and then snaps back to the right to "close" the movement. This final closing happens just upon impact and causes a wave of energy to be thrust into the target.

The voice also plays an important part in all fa-jing. The voice is an intermediary between the physical movement and the internal action. Once again, it gets back to the classics, which say that the breath must be natural. Now most people interpret this to mean that the breath must be slow and constant, but this is wrong. Only if you are performing a slow and constant movement must the breath be such. If you are performing a sudden fa-jing movement, the breath must act accordingly, with an explosive sound emanating from the voice box. This is what is meant by natural breathing—when the breath is in harmony with the movement. So with a fa-jing movement, we cannot use a slow "haaa" sound, for instance; we must use an explosive sound, which can be anything as long as it is explosive (e.g., "ba!" or "pa!").

The next fa-jing action is the "open" fa-jing shake. This is where, in taiji, we use the posture known as "single whip" to strike to no less than four dim-mak points on the neck. This time, the body (assuming that the right palm is doing the work with the right foot forward) shakes first to the left as the right palm attacks to Si 17 (fig. 11), then to the right as the touching fingertips of the right hand attack to Cv 23 (fig. 12) and finally, with this final attack upon St 9 and Si 16 (fig. 13), back to the left, leaving an "open" posture. This type of fa-jing move is said to suck energy away from the opponent.

Figure 11

The third fa-jing action is called "closed up fa-jing shake" and is used to put qi into the points to cause sunstroke or to cause the associated organ to explode. This time the body shakes in the closed way, but there is also an upward spiraling of the body upon impact (fig. 14).

The fourth way of fa-jing, the "open

Figure 12

Figure 13

Figure 14

down fa-jing shake," is used to drain energy from the body. It is the same as the open fa-jing, but with a downward spiraling shake (fig. 15). It is used against Gb 14 to KO.

HOW TO GAIN FA-JING

It's just like sneezing. When you sneeze, you are not able to control your eyes. They must close for that split second. The whole body shakes completely out of control for that split second. This is fa-jing. I have found over the years that the only real obstacle to gaining fa-jing is our own ego. We feel self-conscious and do not wish to be seen "letting go"; we like to appear to be in control at all times. This is the biggest hurdle to overcome —your own mind and ego. Let it go and see what happens. When I hold workshops, I get the whole class to make an explosive sound and allow their whole bodies to shake as they do it. Their feet will even leave the ground as they do it, but their eyes tell the story—glazed and angry, full of energy (qi).

Throw a punch —not the normal closed-fist punch using tension, but rather the internal

Figure 15

loose punch only closing upon impact for that split second. I have people hold their palms so that the palm is facing the floor. Then I show them the explosive sound that can be generated when one whips the palm over to face the ceiling as the fist is closed. A snapping sound is heard if the fa-jing is executed correctly. The feet will leave the ground as it happens.

Then we go on and, still using that same punch, we strike the hard mit only a few centimeters away and see what kind of power is generated. The power is great if the fa-jing is done correctly, with the whole body throwing out the energy upon impact.

As you become more adept at this (well, actually, you either do it or you don't; there is no in between—like saying, "I almost got that touchdown" or "I dug half a hole"), you are able to actually put energy into the points as you strike.

This is the highest level of dim-mak, the putting in of the adverse qi. I can compare this to electricity of very high frequency (VHF or UHF). Special cables are used to carry this sort of electricity because the frequency is so high that when the cable goes around corners, some of the electricity just keeps on going, right out of the cable! It's the same with fa-jing. When we use fa-jing, the power is so great that some qi (electrical energy) is actually sent into the object. We are able to either use this for healing or for the martial arts. This is why it is said that dim-mak takes three lifetimes to master.

CHAPTER THREE

How to Use Dim-Mak

Dim-mak books are few and far between, and those that there are, to my knowledge, do not actually show how to use dim-mak.

All that one gets are a few points and what they do. Dim-mak is a totally integrated fighting system, and it is all one needs to defend oneself. However, if people wish to take from dim-mak the part that most are familiar with (i.e., the points and what they do), then they can take this information and lay it over what they know already.

As I have already stated, dim-mak *is* taiji and, as such, some knowledge of this classical fighting system is imperative in the learning of dim-mak. I do not, of course, expect everyone to take up taiji in order to begin right from scratch. In fact, in most cases this would be detrimental to one's dim-mak training, as not many are teaching taiji as it should be taught. But the following are a few of the training methods I have found very useful to any martial artist, and indeed, in most cases, crucial to training.

THE "C" BACK

The first thing we must know about in dim-mak is the "C" back. I discussed this in the last chapter.

Basically, what it does is get you into an attacking mode. You are just walking down the street, and this raving lunatic attacks you. You don't want to fight; you're just out for a stroll, but he is in full fighting mode, and you must have a way to get into an even better fighting mode. The "C" back does this for you. See Figure 9 in Chapter 2 for the "C" back fighting position or, alternately, Figure 16.

In this posture (fig. 16), you are ready for fighting: your hands are in the fully ready position ("p'eng/ hinge"), but you aren't antagonizing your opponent by actually standing in an "on guard" position. You can talk to him in this position in the hope that he'll calm down, but if he doesn't, you are in the best possible position to fight. The back is slightly bent like the letter "C," like the stance of a gorilla. This stance has the effect of taking us into "the reptilian

Figure 16

brain," which is part of the triune brain. The triune brain is used for survival and is the part we use the least in modern, twentieth-century living. We cannot get this usage in dojo sparring.

By the way, I regard sparring as one of the most harmful games we play in the martial arts. It actually teaches you non-self-defense! We prefer to use "attack/defense" methods in the dojo or dawgwan. This is where the teacher, or someone who has a lot of control, attacks you with all of his might, as if in a street situation. You *know* he is going to hit you if you don't defend yourself, and so you do.

This is where the reptilian part of the brain comes into play to defend you. Some call this qi. All of a sudden, you *have* to defend yourself, and something happens to you, you become an animal. All of a sudden, rather than a soppy guy or girl just walking down the street, the attacker or mugger has this maniac of an animal to contend with, and the tables are turned. It's difficult to use this part of the brain in the classroom, because it is, literally, the survival part, and it is sometimes hard to stop! This is why I stress that only the teacher should do the attacking—and with plenty of protective gear on!

So you go into this posture and you feel something strange rising up to your neck from the backbone—this is the yang energy, ready to explode! Your eyes will become glazed, and often this is enough to tell the attacker's subconscious that you mean business. But if he doesn't stop, then you attack and keep attacking like a wild animal out of control! This is what dim-mak, fa-jing, and this whole fighting system is about—fighting like a wild beast.

Only in the "C" back position can you attain inner stillness, which is one of the taiji classics. Only in this position can you have the shoulders hanging, completely relaxed but alive and ready for action; the chest slightly concave; and the weight shifting internally from foot to foot, without allowing it to show externally. You are still. Isn't this what the taiji classics teach (for those of you who are actually studying taiji)?

Figure 17

Even without great technique, you will have a great deal of success, as this is the fighting position.

P'ENG/HINGE

The classic p'eng/hinge position comes directly from taiji and is the fighting position for the arms (fig. 17). You are ready for anything, and your arms are in a position that will allow you to take any type of attack.

To train in this method, you have your partner throw a straight right initially. As soon as he throws the punch, you just move in—*you must move in!* One of your arms will take the punch and attack as you move in, and/or your other one will also attack (fig. 18). Now you have your partner throw another punch, and you move in again, holding your arms in the same way.

Although you are obviously able to change the position of each arm, for the training method you must keep the left one p'eng (the Chinese word that means

Figure 18

"to ward off slantingly upward") and the right one hinge ("to ward off slantingly downward"), as in Figures 17 and 18. You can move them closer together or move them further apart, and if you do not stop the attack, you are simply doing it wrong.

Do not go out of your way to block; just move in and strike with whatever you have. Later, you will know to strike at the correct points. Figure 19 shows a different attack, against which I have still used the same p'eng/hinge.

EAGLE VISION

To enable you to train in the dim-mak system, it is important to at least try to tell you about "eagle vision." I was teaching a workshop in Australia, and there were a couple of nice karate

Figure 19

chaps there. They were bouncers (doormen) and wanted to know more about their art. When we got to "eagle vision," they were greatly interested but just couldn't get out of the habit of using "focus vision," where they had to first turn and face the oncoming peripheral attack and then do something about it. So I had to invent a training method for them on the spot, and it was one of the greatest revelations they had ever had. They actually learned to look "over there" and still see everything that was going on in front of them, so they got better at seeing the attack before it was launched. This was not using actual eagle vision, but at least they learned how to use their peripheral vision, and this is the start of learning about eagle vision.

Most martial arts tell us something about how we should emulate the actions of animals. We should move like the spritely monkey or pounce like the tiger, and so on. But most importantly, we should have the eye of the eagle ready to strike. When we read this, we usually oversimplify it and just look harder or focus harder. But upon looking further into the Chinese way of the animals in kung-fu, we see that the eagle has a unique system of vision that is exactly how we should be seeing when fighting.

The eagle has a way of literally locking onto its prey—not just the shape of the prey itself but the space that surrounds it as well. We have three types of vision: spot focus, where we look directly at a smaller portion of something and focus upon it; average focus, where we use our total peripheral vision to see the whole subject and surrounding area; and small peripheral focus, where we lock onto the space that the object takes up in the universe. This last type is a very special technique and requires many hours of practice combined with breathing techniques. It enables us to move with the opponent and not wait until he has moved. In other words, we do not see a series of "pictures" as he moves closer and focus separately on these images. Rather, our sight moves as he moves and follows the space that he displaces. A body can only take up the same amount of space, no matter what it is doing and what shape it is placed in (i.e., scrunched up on the floor or standing upright). So if we fight the space displacement then we cannot fail—we move when it moves because we are locked onto that space, and so we adjust our own space accordingly and subconsciously choose the right countermoves and do them automatically.

In order to use "small peripheral vision," we use this simple training method.

Have your partner stand in front of you. Now when I say touch your partner, I don't mean just touch anywhere. You must choose some points, and the best ones are those that will put you in the best position for self-defense. So we usually choose St 9, Gb 14, Si 16, and so on (see the chapter on point location)—the ones that are easiest to get to. But first of all, in order to make sure that you can "see without seeing," look past your partner's shoulder but do not focus on a distant object. Try to keep your mind on your partner's body while your eyes are actually looking past him. You might aim at a distant tree without focusing on it. Poke with your right index finger and see if you can touch your partner's nose right on the tip without having to readjust. Do this as quickly as you can without taking his nose off or sticking your finger up his nose! Your partner can tell you if your eyes move to look at him or if they focus on him.

Now you try to hit (pull) the St 9 points on the neck using the same eye work. Then go to the other easy-to-get-at points, like Gb 14, just above the eyebrow. Once you become accustomed to this, you can increase the speed until you are just touching many of the important points. Go low to Gb 24 and Liv 13 or St 15 and 16.

Then your partner begins to move. He just moves from side to side, and the trick here is to make sure your eyes stay still, aiming at that same spot past him. Keep touching the points as he moves past you, and don't move your eyes. You cannot move your eyes if you are actually looking at your partner with your peripheral vision because you aren't really looking at that tree over there; you are actually seeing your partner, slightly blurred. You cannot make out who it is, but the points are all visible. This exercise will at least take you into peripheral vision.

The next move is to go fully into eagle vision, and this is a little more complicated. To get used to this "moving as he moves," have your partner stand in front of you again. Have him make large movements toward you. Concentrate on seeing his slightest movement. No one can attack you without first of all moving some part of his body, so learn to detect that movement. Go out into the street and, using your peripheral vision, learn to detect movement. See what people are doing and subconsciously try to counter that movement. When your partner moves, you should also move toward him—never backwards! (Part of dim-mak training is learning that we must always move in to strike. There are no blocks; there are, however, blocking strikes.) This throws his timing off and puts you in the most advantageous position.

KICKS

Many people ask me about using kicks with the above methods. The fighting system will not fail you, provided you use the correct actions. Remember that old adage, "If someone attacks you, attack them first"? When we use eagle vision, we never allow anyone to come within our sphere or range of attack. The very instant they do, we attack them! It's as if they have already launched a physical attack on us, and we see it as just that.

Once you have mastered the "C" back, there will be no holding you back anyway; you will want to attack. The very instant the attacker moves, you move in, provided that he is within your range of attack! This is very important, because if you move in to attack too soon, you allow him to know what you are going to do.

Only strike when he is within your range—and if he can hit you, he is in it. This does not mean you look to strike at his face or his center—what about his peripherals? If his arm is within your striking range, then you hit it! If his leg is within your striking range, then you hit it. In order for a person to hit you, you must be able to hit him!

So it's the same with kicks. The very instant he comes within kicking range—and this includes a flying launch or a jumping kick—you move in and attack. This will upset his timing—you were there and now you're not! And you will attack immediately, while his one foot is in the air. He never gets a chance to kick you. Remember, he has to be in range to kick you, so when he comes within range, you don't wait for him to kick—you attack. It doesn't matter if he's the world's fastest kicker; he doesn't get a chance to kick.

THE OPENING TECHNIQUES

It's all very well for me to tell you to attack when he comes within your range, but there are two very useful ways to upset his timing and launch your own surprise attack: the open-sided attack and the closed-sided attack. This is something I always do in workshop. I tell the participants how I will be attacking, and then I stand some feet away and ask them to hold a good on-guard position, perhaps with the hands in the karate-type position, etc. I ask them to try to get away from me when I attack, by either moving backwards or to the side.

So far, no one has been able to escape the dim-mak strike at the end of these attacks. These "opening techniques" can be used either as straight-out attacks when the opponent is deemed to be within your range of attack, or as defensive methods after he has attacked. We'll get on to the "small san-sau methods" shortly.

In order to understand the opening techniques, we have to learn two of the "long har ch'uan" (LHC), or "dragon prawn boxing," methods, as this is where the opening techniques come from. In prawn boxing, your back is in the "C" shape and your arms make like the feelers of a prawn to attack before you are attacked. Your reach is far greater in this position than that of your attacker.

The Vertical Method

Your partner stands in front of you and attacks with a straight right. You are standing in the normal boxing position with one foot (doesn't matter which) slightly forward. You "block" his attack using your right palm, slapping his arm on a point called "neigwan," or Pc 6 (see the chapter on points), toward you as if you are brushing away flies (fig. 20).

Notice the position of the other hand. It is already coming up to take over that blocking strike. Why not simply use the left hand in the beginning?

Another principle of dim-mak fighting is that we never allow our internal "nice" instincts to overtake what we are trying to do. Deep down, we all want to help each other. Even if we are intent on fighting, this is a subconscious thing in all human beings . . . well, most of us! So when we throw a punch and it is blocked, we subcon-

Figure 20

sciously slack off and begin with the other hand. This is how many schools teach self-defense. But look at the leverage advantage you have, especially if your opponent blocks using that left hand (fig. 21). You are able to punch right through that block if you are really intent on hitting the target and you are not slacking off. I'm talking about a real punch here—not using the arm alone, but the whole body.

So you have successfully defended and also hurt your opponent's arm and caused a rush of qi to be routed to that point. This is what neigwan does—it is a classic set-up point, leaving the more dangerous points more vulnerable. (Neigwan by itself, by the way, will cause someone to feel very ill and

Figure 21

perhaps turn a little green! So turn the arm over and tap three times down the arm in exactly the opposite spot on the back of the arm and this will fix it.)

There are only two movements but four sounds heard in LHC. You have just heard the first sound and begun the first movement, turning your body to your left and sitting back slightly. Now, as your left palm takes over the

Figure 22

block, your right palm slams down on your opponent's second attack to your lower right ribs. Your left palm slams down into the crease of his elbow, as in Figure 22, and causes nerve damage. The second sound was your left palm taking over the block, while the third sound was your right palm slamming into his elbow. This is the first body movement. You have basically turned to your left and sat back. His second attack could have been a high hook punch, which is the first peripheral movement of this exercise (fig. 23).

Now, the second movement: as you move your weight onto your forward foot, turn your waist to the front and slam your opponent's face with your left palm or chest. This is the fourth sound (fig. 24). Again, you should hear four distinct sounds here. If you only hear two, then you're doing it incorrectly. You should not use both hands for the initial block, nor should you block the second attack with your right palm and attack with your left simultaneously.

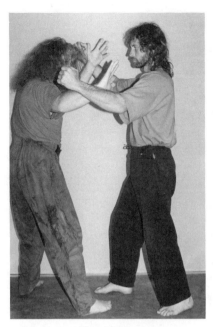

Figure 23

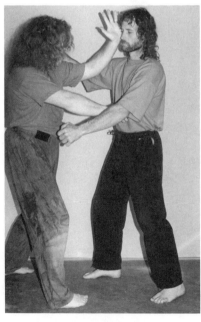

Figure 24

This has been an "open sided movement." Once you have learned this side, you do it on the other side, of course, with the same footing. So you get four different ways to do it: right foot forward, right-sided; right foot forward, left-sided; and vice versa.

It will only take a split second to execute this whole technique with your partner throwing very fast punches. It's important for your partner to throw the second punch very soon after the first one, as you cannot wait. You must attack with your final blow, even if he hesitates with his second punch. In this case, your attacking right palm will only guard his left arm as your left palm crashes onto his face or chest.

So a good training method is to have your partner

not throw his second punch or wait. You still have to do your own thing and not wait for his second punch.

Step Up, Parry, and Punch

The second of the dragon prawn boxing methods uses the taiji postures known as "step up, parry, and punch." Your partner attacks with a straight right again. You step to your left and attack his forearm on Colon 10 with your right backfist (fig. 25). Your left hand immediately slams Co 12, just above his right elbow (fig. 26) and then continues to his neck at Si 16. Your right palm now attacks his left St 9 point, while your left hand takes over the right punch (fig. 27). This is also done on the other side.

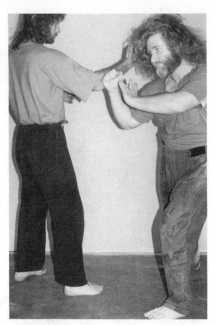

Figure 25

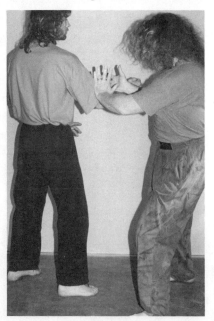

Figure 26

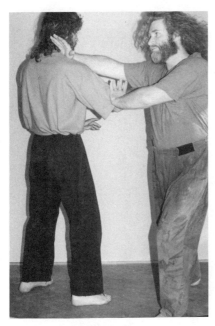

Figure 27

Figure 28

Open-Sided Opening Technique

Here, you will learn how to open up on your opponent's open side. Your partner stands in front of you. You move around a bit. When he comes within your striking range, you will use the vertical LHC method first. Slam his lead hand at neigwan as your other palm takes over the block (fig. 28). Your first hand now slams his other arm into his body or just slams it.

Your second hand is now free to attack St 9 (fig. 29). It must be said that this method will not work if fa-jing is not used. Your body must explode into action so that your opponent doesn't have any idea what is happening.

This works because your opponent expects you

to attack in a certain way—with a hook, a straight, a kick, and so on. So he is not ready for the attack to neigwan, which causes all of his energy and concentration to go to that point. He is taken completely off guard, and at that moment, when all of his energy is scattered, all of a sudden his arm is being slammed into his body, while your

Figure 29

hand is slamming St 9, knocking him out. It's a complete shock; even when you tell people what is about to happen, they are still not ready for it.

The first attack to neigwan must be a fa-jing explosive attack accompanied by a cracking sound. If you just push your opponent's arm out of the way, he will register this and have time to readjust.

I get a little tired of people talking about "long-range martial arts" and "short-range martial arts." How can there be such a thing as a long-range art? No one can hit you unless they are within range anyway! Fighting takes place when the attacker is able to hit you, and that means he's fairly close.

Closed-Sided Opening Technique

Your partner stands in front of you and again holds the on-guard position. This time, and only when he comes within range, slam the outside of his arm at Co 10 (fig. 30). This is the shock. Before

Figure 30

he realizes it, your other hand has again shocked him by slamming into Co 12, just above the elbow, and is now controlling that arm (fig. 31), leaving your right palm free to strike St 9 to knock him out (fig. 32).

SMALL SAN-SAU

This method comes directly from the Yang Shou-hou side of the Yang family and is an excellent way to learn about some of the main points used in dim-mak.

The most important thing to remember here is not to strike at, for instance, the shoulder, as opposed to the actual point, in order "to get a more realistic feel." It is much better to aim at the real target but pull the strike just short of it. Striking parts other than the points will get you into that mode, and

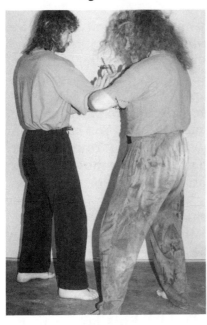

Figure 31

in a real situation, because you have trained to strike there, that's where you *will* strike, sure as eggs. So aim for the real points, but *please* pull the strikes, as these points are really dangerous!

Figure 32

Never do we actually strike two points simultaneously. This works sometimes when using a very basic dim-mak strike to very dangerous points. But to execute the real dim-mak, we must strike the points just a split second after each other. In this way, the qi is going here, then there, and thus upsetting the whole balance of the internal workings (the flow of qi).

It looks as if you are striking two points at once because it is so fast and explosive. You stand with your feet shoulder-width apart. Your partner throws a right hook to the head (the most common street-type attack, apart from a gun or knife). You swivel on your heels.

Why? The wing chun people always ask me this, as they are usually told to swivel on their toes. Swiveling on the toes is for evasion, while swiveling on the heels is for power. For this exercise, we need the most power possible because the attack is so powerful. To demonstrate this point, have your partner hold his hook punch, stopped about 12 inches away from your head. Put out your left wrist and touch his arm. Now, swivel on your toes (moving your heels to the right). See how your right palm is now pulled away from the inside of his wrist; you would have to extend your hand in order to keep touching it. Now swivel on your heels, thus leaving your center where it was and moving your toes to your left. See how your hand has stayed there, touching his wrist; you have not had to move your arm.

It's important that your left arm swing out to your left upon impact of your opponent's punch. Do not use the old "upper block." It's also important that the striking area of your palm is that hard-boned bit on the right side of your left palm when it's facing you (fig. 33). Do not strike with your ulna—it will break! Many a Kyokoshin warrior received a broken ulna because of the old upper block.

Slam this area into his neigwan point on the inside of your partner's right forearm. This will only work if he is actually able to hit you, so get the distance right to begin with. We sometimes begin with a newspaper rolled around the forearms until they build up and you are able to protect your own points. (Remember, never strike bone on bone; this only damages you.)

Your right palm is thrust straight out into your

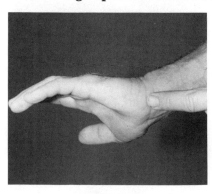

Figure 33

opponent's St 9 points almost simultaneously (fig. 34). This combination of St 9 and Pc 6 is devastating —it is a death strike. So please, do not allow your strikes to come anywhere near your partner. The first move drains while the next one stops the heart. You first swivel to your left, striking his right inner arm and attacking to his neck with your right palm. Then he throws a left hook punch and you repeat the whole routine to your right. Then you return to the initial side and do it all again.

Now your partner throws a left hook to your right ribs. The back of your left forearm swings down as your right palm slams down onto your own Co 10 points. If this is done correctly it will slam into his H 6 and Lu 5 points to cause great qi drainage (fig. 35). Now, immediately and without changing your weight, you bounce off of your left foot and step forward. You should strike into

Figure 34

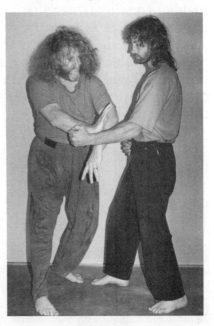

Figure 35

Figure 36

the "mind point" (a special point used in acupuncture to stop the signals from getting from the central nervous system to the brain) with your left backfist. All you have to do here is aim the back of your wrist into the chin. When you whip your arm back, the knuckles of your left fist will whip out onto the side of your opponent's jaw.

Just before this, however, you must use a "negative strike" to his left wrist, thus further affecting his heart and lung points. It is not a pull, but an explosive jerking movement against the wrist bones using fa-jing from your waist (fig. 36). Now what does this look like? The posture known as p'eng from the basic taiji form. In fact, this small san-sau teaches the use of the postures up to the "single whip" posture.

Now your partner attacks low to your left side, so you should still swivel to your left on your right heel as you bring your left foot back to where the other one is and simultaneously perform the technique you just did (fig. 37).

You bounce forward again as before, only this time the technique is different. Your right backfist is more vertical and attacks Cv 24 at a downward angle. A normal backfist will do this anyway because of the action of the fist and the arm held in this way. However, just before this strike, your left palm scrapes violently up the inside of your partner's right arm and ends up striking Sp 20 on the front of his shoulder. This is the set-up point strike and is very energy adding, so that the Cv 24 strike will be like an explosion into his head (fig. 38).

Next, your partner throws a left rip to your right ribs. You turn your left palm up, and as you again swivel on your left heel to bring back your left foot, you slam your left palm down onto his Co 12 point in a direction that is toward you. (Be careful here, as this can incapacitate his arm for some time.) As you do this, however, your right forearm is scissored underneath your own left forearm to stop any further attack with this same hand (fig. 39).

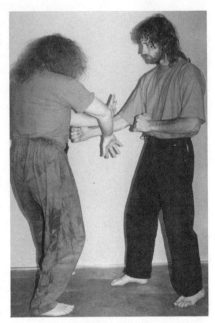

Figure 37

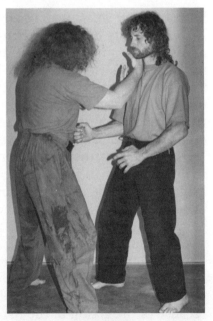

Figure 38

Figure 39

You are now going to perform a simple swivel to the left side as you draw in both of your arms like scissors opening up, still held in that same position. As you fully turn to meet his right rip to your left ribs, you thrust out both forearms like scissors closing to slam heart and lung points on the inside of his inner forearm (fig. 40).

Now, almost instantaneously, you bounce forward with your right foot and, placing your left palm on the inside of your right wrist, attack his Liv 14, as in Figure 41. (Careful here, as this is very dangerous.) It's not a push, but rather a fa-jing shake—a strike. The palms do not just strike as they are, though. Here, you must release yin and yang energy simultaneously.

Figure 40

To do this, you begin with your palms as in Figure 42, the left one being yin-shaped and full of yang qi, while the right one is yang-shaped and full of yin qi. To release these respective energies into the point, you should explosively change the state of each palm as it makes contact, making an explosive sound like "pa!" as you strike (fig. 43).

Figure 41

Next, your partner throws a straight left to your face, and you immediately swivel your right foot back, turning to your right on your left heel as your right palm scrapes toward you on his neigwan. This is the set-up point. As you do this, your left

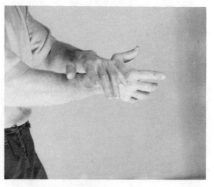

Figure 42

palm has turned over and has struck H 3 on his left forearm (careful here), as in Figure 44.

Now, without stopping (this whole change step should only take a split second; remember, the front foot must come back first, then the other foot steps—don't just jump and change feet), you step forward

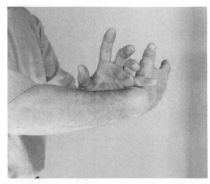

Figure 43

with your left foot and, flicking your left fist over, strike under his chin.

The action of this sort of punch will naturally send your fist upward as it closes upon impact. This is a dangerous "nerve strike," causing the whole nervous system to go into spasm (fig. 45).

Your partner now throws two more straight punches, and you respond in exactly the same way, only you start on the left side and end up attacking with your right fist and then return to the first side, again ending up as in Figure 45.

Figure 44

Now your opponent attacks with a straight right again. This time the technique begins the same way, only you do not step. Swiveling back on your right heel, you slam his right inner wrist at neigwan and strike H 3 exactly the same way, then perform the same punch but without the step. The weight is on your right foot (fig. 46). Now, as you swivel to your right on both heels, you violently thrust his right arm in a downward arc over to your right and catch it with your right hand (fig. 47). Using the momentum of that movement, you step in with your left foot and attack his Gb 24 with your left forearm or fist (fig. 48). You should use extreme caution here, as this is a death strike when done heavily and a KO if done with medium force.

Figure 45

The reverse is now performed. Your opponent throws a straight left and you take it with your right palm as you sit back. This time you do not attack H 3, but rather swivel straight away, while bringing your left foot back and thrusting your opponent's left arm over to your left, catching it with your left palm. You now

Figure 46

Figure 47

Figure 48

step in and perform the exact same technique to Gb 24 as in Figure 48, but on the reverse side.

Now your opponent attacks you with both palms, perhaps trying to choke you. You should not swivel this time, but rather bring your right foot back and, opening up both forearms on the inside of both of his arms, attack Gv 25 using the side of your forehead. In other words, smash him in the nose using the old head-butt (fig. 49)! Now, as you step in with your left foot, take both your palms and, turning them outward to hold up both of his arms, attack both sides of his pectorals at St 15 and St 16, using a twisting motion of the palms. Your right palm will turn clockwise while the left does the reverse. The turning must happen after the palms have touched. *Be careful, as this strike done in this direction stops the heart* (fig. 50)!

This time your partner has something to do, so he brings his left forearm under and blocks your left arm upward before you get there. He now attacks with a punch or finger jab to your left arm. You sit back and immediately swivel on your right heel, bringing your left foot back and swiveling to your left as your right forearm drops down onto your left, thus stopping the attack (fig. 51). Now you swivel to your right on both heels, pulling his right arm over to your right. As you do this, your left palm slides up under the

Figure 49

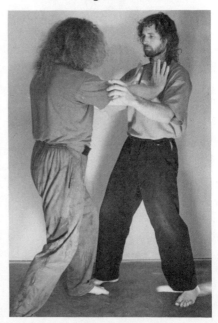

Figure 50

Figure 51

inside of your right elbow (fig. 52). You now bounce forward on your left foot as your left knife edge attacks Gb 3 (temple) with a lifting motion. Never strike using the knife edge when the fingers are all touching (i.e., be sure to open them up), as this will cause percussive breaks in your fingers. The palm must flick upward upon impact (fig. 53).

He again attacks to your right axilla, so you perform the same technique, sitting back with your left arm on top of your right arm this time. You then swivel to your left and pull his left arm over to your right, stepping with your right foot and again attacking Gb 3 with the knife edge of your right palm.

(Now we are using a very useful weapon. Not many will be able to tell

Figure 52

you how to use this "hook," as shown in Figure 54—they always say it's for hooking! Or for pecking! Neither is correct.)

He now attacks your left lower rib area with a right rip. You slam the left side of your hooked palm down onto his forearm, striking at either neigwan or lung points on the thumb side of his forearm; either will cause great pain and energy drainage. The direction here is straight in (fig. 55). Now you swivel to your right while bringing your right foot back and throw his right arm violently over to your right and out of the way. Notice the position of the left palm (fig. 56). It's there to guard for the next technique.

Figure 53

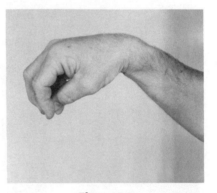

Figure 54

Now, you bounce forward on your left foot as you attack straight in and downward using the knuckles of your right, still hooked hand. Please note that this strike must not be directed straight in, as you will hurt your wrist by bending it. Rather, the direction of

Figure 55

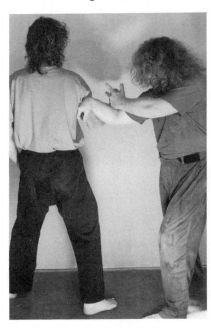

Figure 56

the knuckles must be downward. The knuckles must scrape down under his arm, thus striking at a number of important points, including Gb 22 and Liv 21. This is very energy draining. The left hand is there to stop any further attack by the right hand (fig. 57).

Next your opponent throws a straight left. You sit back and slam his inner forearm upward using your right hook. You then take the hook over the top of his right arm and swivel to your right, bringing your left foot back as you do. His left arm is thrust violently over to your left, and you come forward with the same technique (fig. 58). The only difference is that you are now in a "natural stance," whereas before you were in a reverse stance.

Next he throws

a right straight, and you again slam it upward with your right hook. But this time you step back with your right foot and move into him, hooking your right hook over his right wrist as your left palm comes down just above his right elbow (fig. 59). Now, because you have moved in, he is unable to escape as you lock his wrist with your right hook, pulling his now bent wrist in to your stomach. If you do this correctly, he cannot pull away even if you only hold him with this one hand. All you have to do now is to turn your body to your right and lean forward a bit to break his wrist and drain energy from his heart and lungs. You can use the left palm to Tw 12 to further assist in this technique

Figure 57

Figure 58

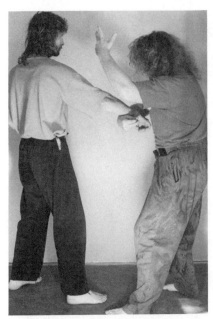

Figure 59

Figure 60

(fig. 60). Your left foot has to come forward with no weight placed on it, as it is used to kick to his lower leg if necessary.

You allow him to escape, of course, so that you can continue. He attacks with a straight left as you again slam it from underneath with your right hooked palm. Roll the hook over the top of his left wrist again, and as you swivel to your left and bring your left foot back, thrust his left arm over to your right and out of the way. Now step in with your right foot and attack his bladder points on either side of his backbone with your right palm. This is the classic "single whip posture," the reverse of Figure 62.

Now he attacks with a straight right, so you sit back and slam his neigwan with your right palm. This can be very painful, so take it easy (fig. 61). The right hook again goes over the top of his right wrist, and, as you swivel over to your right bringing your right foot back, you thrust his right arm violently over to your right and out of the way. Now you step forward with your left foot and again attack the bladder points with your left palm (fig. 62).

Finally, you bow and say thanks to each other. The above is an excellent training method to get into the mode of striking specific points, rather than just striking any-where. Write down all of the points mentioned and learn where they are. Then try them out in the above exercise, trying to relate the tech-

Figure 61

Figure 62

nique to the point. This way, you will remember where the points are because of the physical way of doing small san-sau.

(My third video teaches this exercise, along with large san-sau and pauchui form.)

CHAPTER FOUR

The Points and What They Do

As I mentioned previously, much of the healing information in this book was taken from the *Point Location and Point Dynamics Manual*. Although complete instruction of the dim-mak martial art includes healing information, this manual is a little more scientific and precise than the original dim-mak texts and translations, so I decided to consult it as well on the healing side.

In this chapter, I will list the main dim-mak points and explain what they do in the martial sense. (I will assume that you already know the abbreviated names for the points from studying the previous chapters. For the techniques for using these points and instruction on how to get in to use them, see the following chapter.) In each case, the antidotes to use when someone has been struck in these points will follow.

For those acupuncture points that are of special significance to us in the martial arts and those used as antidotes for martial arts injuries, I will first give the healing applications. It's very important for martial artists to know about healing; the martial arts should be totally integrated with the healing arts. As we are already using "points," it is not too difficult to learn about these points for healing also. Many people ask me about the two different types of energy we put in, either to heal or to kill. All that matters here is what is in your mind at the time of application. For the fighting art, the qi will be adverse; for the healing art, the qi will be positive.

(For the complete healing art of taiji, see my video entitled *T'ai Chi Healing & Iron Shirt Qigong*, which shows what each posture does in the healing area.)

Bladder 6

Martial. This point, on the side of head and slightly to the front, 1 cun from centerline, takes away energy from rest of body when struck from front to back.

Antidote. Sit in a crouched position and rub the point from the back of the head to the front.

Bladder 10

Martial. Located on both sides of the neck just below the bottom of the ear and about 1 cun from either side of the spine, Bl 10 is the old rabbit chop and is very dangerous. It takes energy away from the lower heater or kidneys, and if struck straight in it will cause kidney failure. In addition, it will cause extreme knockout and can result in a broken neck. A light strike to this point can cause extreme light-headedness and also emotional problems later in life.

Antidote. Massage Kidney 1 point straight in.

Also massage either side of the backbone from the tailbone to the lower neck gently in an upward way.

Colon 10 (LARGE INTESTINE)

Martial. Striking this point on the outside of the forearm in at an upward angle causes nausea and lack of energy in the lower body.

Antidote. Squeeze Co 1 at the tip of the index finger on the outside, just at the joining of the fingernail.

Martial. Striking Co 10 at a downward angle causes extreme colon activity and literally causes someone to shit themselves!

Antidote. Rub Co 10 *lightly* in a downward way using the thumb, and squeeze Co 1.

Martial. When struck straight in, Co 10 will cause spasm of the whole lower abdomen area and "dead arm."

Antidote. Rub the whole outside of the forearm in a downward way again, away from the body, using the knuckles and a little more pressure than for the last antidote. The arm should come back to life very quickly and the spasms should stop, though there will be some residual diarrhea.

Colon 12

Martial. When struck at a downward angle, this point, just above the elbow on the outside of forearm, will cause all energy to be drained from the body.

Antidote. Rub the point toward you gently but with deep penetration.

Conceptor Vessel 4

Healing. Cv 4, or tan tien (3 cun below the navel on the midline), is a "mu" point for the small intestine, meaning it is directly above it. It promotes the function of the kidneys and strengthens them. It also increases the yang energy, serving as a major tonification point for the whole body.

Martial. When struck in a downward direction,

Cv 4 drains the energy from the whole body.

Antidote. Massage middle tan tien gently or apply light upward pressure to Cv 1. Also use Gv 26, using light upward pressure to increase the flow of qi.

Martial. To increase the blood pressure, strike or kick Cv 4 in an upward direction. This can be fatal in a person whose blood pressure is already sky-high.

Anidote. Rub the point downward to bring blood pressure down, or tweak Stomach 9 to cause the carotid sinus to react.

Martial. When struck straight in, Cv 4 causes blackout and a total slowing of qi. It is very dangerous.

Antidote. Lay the person in the coma position. Massage the top of the head at Gv 21 and rub the whole chest area in a downward direction.

Conceptor Vessel 6

Healing. Cv 6, 1.5 cun below the navel, regulates the circulation of qi and is another major tonification point for the whole body.

Martial. When struck straight in, Cv 6 also causes the blood pressure to rise.

Antidote. The antidote is the same as that used for Cv 4.

Conceptor Vessel 14

Healing. Cv 14 calms the heart, mind, and spirit, pacifies the stomach, and balances the qi. It is used to clear up conditions—especially those that deal with disruptive qi above the diaphragm, such as vomiting, coughing, hiccoughing, etc.—which have become chronic and therefore dangerous.

Martial. Located just over the xiphoid process and 7 cun superior to the navel on the midline, this is a heart mu point and is therefore extremely dangerous! When struck straight in, death occurs instantly.

Antidote. There is no remedy other than trying CPR.

Martial. When struck at a downward angle, this takes the energy away from the lungs, making us feel like we have taken the old "kick in the guts."

Antidote. We must use CPR or some other method of getting the lungs to work again. At the same time, we should lightly rub H 3 backward toward the armpit.

Martial. Striking Cv 14 in at an upward angle causes external damage and energy topping (i.e., putting too much energy into the point, causing overaction of the organ).

Antidote. Use St. 9, but be careful because this is a knockout point, remember? Gently massage St 9 until the heart rate has ceased to be dangerously low.

Conceptor Vessel 17

Healing. Used for asthma, chest pain, and insufficient lactation (papaws are also good for this), this point (between the nipples on the midline) regulates the circulation of qi, soothes the diaphragm, and clears the lungs.

Martial. Both the lungs and the diaphragm control the seat of power in the human body, so striking this point at a downward angle causes the seat of power to leave and the person falls to the ground. It can seem quite funny, but it isn't!

Antidote. Push with a thumb into Cv 17 in an upward way, using a fair amount of pressure. This will bring the energy back into the diaphragm.

Martial. Striking Cv 17 at an upward angle causes spasm in the lower body.

Antidote. Apply pressure to the same point in a downward way.

Conceptor Vessel 22

Healing. This point is used to cure cough and asthma and when suppressed emotions, such as fear or grief, are contributing to asthma. It can disperse obstructed lung qi and harmonize the relationship between the pericardium and the spleen.

Martial. This is an extreme death point just in the pit of the neck. It is struck inward only, with the sole purpose of causing death.

Antidote. There is no antidote point for this other than CPR.

Conceptor Vessel 24

Healing. This point, just under bottom lip on the indent, controls rebellious stomach qi and is used to help cure nausea.

Martial. A finger strike from left to right will cause nausea, vomiting, and blackout.

Antidote. Rub the tan tien (Cv 4) in a counter-clockwise direction in a small circle. If he has been attacked from his right to left, causing loss of balance and hearing, rub Cv 4 in a clockwise direction in a small circle.

Martial. Striking this point straight inward will knock the teeth out!

Antidote. Fix the teeth!

Conceptor Vessel 14 and Conceptor Vessel 4

Martial. Striking these two points straight in, almost simultaneously—as in the "double dragon strike" (fig. 63) from Bagwazhang—will cause death if the strike is strong enough. A mild strike will cause serious knockout. Here we use a straight-in strike.

Antidote. There are no points for this one; use CPR.

Gall Bladder 1

Healing. Gb 1, located at the corner of the eye, will strengthen the eyes and is good for headache. It connects to the liver and promotes the free flow of qi.

Martial. Striking at this point in a direction from the back of the head to the front will cause nausea at the very least and loss of memory or death at

most. The tips of the fingers are used to scrape this point.

Antidote. Rub Gb 1 backward toward the back of the head on both sides. Press Gv 26, just under the nose, lightly inward. CPR will not work unless the antidote points have been used.

Martial. Striking Gb 1 from rear to front in combination with a straight-in strike to Cv 22 will cause death instantly.

Figure 63

Antidote. There is no cure.

Gall Bladder 3
Healing. Gb 3 is used for tinnitus and facial palsy.
Martial. If the temple is struck straight inward very hard, death occurs immediately and nothing will revive the person. If the strike was not hard enough to cause instant death but internal bleeding is suspected, keep him quiet and get him to the hospital without fail, as death will occur within three days if internal bleeding is let go!
Antidote. There is no antidote.

Gall Bladder 14
Healing. This point, in the middle of the eyebrow, is used for healing blurred vision, twitching of the eyelids, and frontal headache. It connects to the triple warmer and colon meridians.
Martial. Striking it in a downward way to cause

THE POINTS AND WHAT THEY DO   91

energy drainage results in knockout if the hit is not too hard and death if it is very hard. Usually the palm is used to strike at this point.

Antidote. Use Gb 20, at the base of the skull on both sides, pressing upward into the skull. Also use Gb 21, on the trapezium, pressing straight down. If the heart stops, use CPR immediately.

Martial. Striking it an upward manner will cause a yang energy rush to the head, resulting in extreme dizziness and eventual death. This is the same as giving someone an extreme case of sunstroke.

Antidote. Push Gb 21 away from the neck toward the outer shoulder on both sides. This will bring the yang energy out and put yin energy in. Also rub Gb 20 in a downward way toward the base of the neck. In addition, press inward on Si 4, just over the wristband in the little hollow on the outside of wrist, with medium pressure. Use CPR in the event of death or near death. (Now you also know how to treat someone with sunstroke!)

Martial. Striking straight inward at this point will cause knockout, as it will prevent signals from getting through to the brain.

Antidote. If the person's neck is broken, he must be taken to the hospital! If he is completely "out of it" (disorientated, eyes glazed, tongue hanging out and swelling), rub downward at Gb 14 (not too hard) and Gb 21. Give him water to drink as he comes back. If he blacks out and breathing and heart have stopped, apply CPR.

Gall Bladder 22

Healing. Gb 22 is used to strengthen the heart.

Martial. Striking under the arm straight into Gb 22 (3 cun below the anterior axillary fold in the fourth intercostal space) will cause the heart to falter or stop.

Antidote. Massage H 3 or Co 10 straight in with light pressure.

Gall Bladder 24

Healing. This point is used to eliminate "damp heat." It strengthens the middle heater to promote the transformation of fluids, eliminating dampness.

Martial. Located on the seventh intercostal space in line with the nipples, this point, when struck straight in, will cause knockout by action of the carotid sinus. If struck in combination with Liv 14, or by itself with enough power, it can be a death point. At the least it will debilitate and at most it will kill.

Antidote. If the person is shaking uncontrollably, or if knockout has occurred, massage the Gb 20 points on either side of the neck. If death is near, medical treatment is needed.

Gall Bladder 31

Healing. Gb 31 relaxes the tendons and strengthens the waist and knees. It is also used for shingles and for the after-effects of stroke.

Martial. This point is located on the outside of the leg, right where the fingers hang to when the arms are extended. A straight-in strike here will paralyze the leg and, when used along with a wrist attack, cause knockout.

Antidote. Rub Gb 31 in a downward way.

Governor Vessel 20

Healing. Gv 20 clears the mind by harmonizing the yang energy. It can restore yang energy to the head by drawing on the reserves of the body. It is a major revival point.

Martial. BEWARE! This point, at the top of the head, is an extreme death point. A light strike here will cause knockout and extreme energy drainage from the lower heating area, and the legs, etc., will go, then the mind (i.e., extreme disorientation). All of the qi for the whole system flows up to and through Gv 20, so it is a major dim-mak point.

However, it is not a very easy matter to get at this point, especially if the person is tall.

Antidote. Massage Gv 20 inward gently. Press Co 10 hard so that the person flinches if still awake. This will bring the energy back to the lower body and also to the Gv 20 point.

Governor Vessel 26

Healing. This is also a classic revival point. It is like giving someone smelling salts on an internal level. It calms the mind and relaxes the whole body.

Martial. Just under the nose, this very sensitive area can cause death if struck hard. It is very good to teach women or smaller people to strike in an upward way into the upper tooth ridge.

Antidote. Here we are using another classic revival point to cure a revival point that has been struck. If a straight-up strike causes knockout and not death, hold your palm over Gv 20 using light pressure. This should bring the person around. If not, then also use the yuyao (fish's belly) point, on the eyebrow just above the pupil (if the person is looking straight ahead). Push this point in and downward.

Heart 1

Martial. This point is difficult to get to, but a strike straight up into the armpit to H 1 will cause the heart to stop.

Antidote. There is really no antidote other than CPR, though you might try squeezing the little finger at H 9.

Heart 3

Martial. Heart 3, in the crease of the elbow, is another very dangerous point. Strike it toward you, away from the normal flow of energy, to prevent the heart from receiving energy and thus causing it to stop.

Antidote. There is not much that can be done, but you could try rubbing H 3 with the flow of qi (back up the arm toward the shoulder) or squeezing the little finger on the inside at the tip (H 9), which will take yang qi to the heart and possibly revive it.

Martial. If struck away from you, this results in extreme heart activity and very high blood pressure.

Antidote. Tweak St 9 carefully. This causes the carotid sinus to react, which slows the extreme heart activity. If the heart has stopped (which can occur if H 3 is struck in either direction), CPR is recommended.

Martial. Striking H 3 straight inward weakens the heart but causes more external damage because it is also a nerve-point strike which will damage the nerves on the inside of the upper arm. This is a nasty strike, as the receiver does not know that his heart has been affected.

Antidote. Squeeze H 9 each evening and morning.

Heart 5

Martial. Striking this point (1 cun above wrist flexure on the ulna artery, toward the thumb side) toward you will take away energy from your opponent's body and lower his blood pressure.

Antidote. Gently rub H 5 toward you and massage H 3 straight in.

Heart 5 and Lung 8

Martial. These points, on the inside of the wrist on either side about 1 cun back from the wrist flexure, will cause the heart and lungs to be affected if struck straight in, as in a block.

If these points are pulled toward you, it will cause the body to lose energy fast, creating an opening for a follow-up strike.

Antidote. Gently massage the Heart 5 and Lung 6 points toward you. This applies both when the points are struck straight in and when they are pulled toward you.

Kidney 5

Healing. K 5 is used to relieve pain around the umbilicus and is one of the classic menstrual pain points.

Martial. Striking this point on the Achilles tendon at a downward angle (for instance, with the heel stomp on the back of the tendon) using the taiji posture called "single whip" will cause dizziness and disorientation and, if the strike is heavy, fainting. It will also cause damage to the kidneys, and blood will appear in the urine. Medical attention should be sought.

Antidote. Squeeze K 5 in from both sides gently. Also massage K 1.

Liver 6

Martial. Striking Liv 6 (middle of leg between the knee and ankle on the inside of the calf, slightly to the front of the leg and back from the tibia) and K 9 (1 cun back from the tibia and a little less than halfway up the leg) in combination with Pc 6 and H 3 (as with the pa-kua method of opening up using the feet as well) will cause extreme confusion, thus setting up for a more potent strike.

Antidote. Press K 5 and K 1, then rub the forearms in the positive energy directions (i.e., down the outside of the forearm and up the inside).

Liver 13

Martial. This point is at the side of the waist, toward the front a bit, at the tip of the free end of the eleventh rib. Striking Liv 13 straight in will cause vomiting, diarrhea, and lack of power in the lower body, as well as emotional disturbances.

Antidote. Massage Liv 14 gently inward. Also try Liv 3. If emotional disturbances are occurring as a delayed reaction to a strike here, you should massage Lung 3, on the lateral side of the biceps, just down from the armpit.

Liver 14

Martial. Striking the right point from left to right and vice versa causes extreme liver problems and can cause blindness.

Antidote. Massage Liv 14 (just under the nipple where the pectorals make a crease) in the opposite direction of the strike and massage Liv 3, just between the big and second toes. Massage Gv 20, at the top of head and slightly back from Gv 21.

Martial. When struck straight in, Liv 14 causes emotional problems, including extreme anxiety. It also causes the lungs to cave in.

Antidote. If emotional problems occur some time after being struck, massage Liv 14 straight inward gently. If the lungs have caved in, seek medical assistance at a hospital—this can be deadly.

Liver 8 and Conceptor Vessel 2

Martial. Striking Liv 8 (to the left of the knee crease on the back of the right leg and vice versa) first causes severe liver as well as genital damage. You can use this to block a kick using both arms and then come in with the elbow to Cv 2. A strike to Liv 8 becomes more deadly when combined with Cv 2.

Antidote. Treat kidney points K 1 and K 5, as well as Bl 23, located in the back just over both kidneys. Press K 1 inward on the sole of the feet until mild pain is felt. Grab K 5 with the thumb and forefinger on either side of the Achilles tendon and squeeze gently to the point of pain. Apply light pressure to Bl 23, pressing straight inward using the thumb.

Lung 3

Healing. This point is used to treat asthma and epistaxis (nosebleed).

Martial. Located on the outside of the biceps just below the shoulder, this one is easy to get at. A strike here upsets the balance of energy between mind and body. Extreme sadness is felt as a result, but the person is unable to express it because of the blockage created by the strike, and he may experience extreme depression over a long period if not treated. Vertigo is another effect of being struck here.

Antidote. Treat the point with mild pressure, massaging inward toward you.

The Mind Point (Qianzheng)

Martial. The mind point is just at the hinge of the jaw where there is a "little fat bit." Fiddle around until you find a sore spot when pressing back toward the backbone. This is called a "new point" (one discovered as the science of acupuncture progressed which did not connect to any of the known meridians or channels) and, like the fish's belly, has no particular meridian. It is called the knockout point because when struck from the front to the rear and inward it interrupts the signals to the brain from the central nervous system and thus results in knockout.

Antidote. Squeeze Gb 20 lightly and rub the point back toward the chin. This will usually bring the person around after a short wait.

Martial. Striking this point straight inward is a little more serious, as this can cause complete knockout and eventual death.

Antidote. Rub both Gb 3 points (temples) toward you, counterclockwise on his left side and clockwise on his right side. Then use a slight slap downward onto his Gb 21s. Apply CPR in the event of a serious knockout.

Mind Point and Governor Vessel 26

Martial. Striking this point to the rear while

striking Gv 26 straight in results in severe central nervous system damage, causing the person to quiver on the ground.

Antidote. If there is one, it would be to rub H 7, or shenmen, back toward the shoulder.

Neigwan

Martial. This easily accessible point, also known as Pc 6, is a very dangerous one. A strike toward you to this point (about 2 cun up from the wrist flexure in the middle of the inside of the forearm between the radius and the ulna) will affect the heart, causing it to miss a few beats or even stop completely. This point also controls the balance of yin and yang in the body and will therefore upset the whole balance of the body when struck.

Antidote. Turn the wrist over and gently knock Triple Warmer 5 and 6 (directly opposite of Pc 6) three times in a toward-you direction.

Martial. When struck straight in, this point causes extreme nausea and lack of power in the lower body.

Antidote. Rub the same point in the opposite direction of the strike.

Martial. When struck in an away-from-you direction, this point will cause the mind to become scattered.

Antidote. Rub the point lightly in the same direction as the strike.

Neigwan and Stomach 9

Martial. When attacked in combination with Stomach 9, Pc 6 is very dangerous. The first strike takes the qi to neigwan, leaving St 9 vulnerable to a follow-up strike.

Antidote. Grab Gb 20 and squeeze.

Neigwan and Triple Warmer 8

Martial. Striking Pc 6 and Tw 8 (in the middle of

the back of the forearm), one after the other, and then striking across the Cv 24 point will cause irreversible damage to the heart and internal energy system, resulting in death some years later.

Antidote. None.

Neigwan and Triple Warmer 12

Martial. Tw 12 is located just where the horseshoe is on the triceps. Striking this point straight in immediately following a neigwan strike will cause paralysis of the arm.

Antidote. Stroke the point toward you.

Stomach 9

Martial. This is the classic knock-out point. Some egotistical martial artists use it to great effect in demonstration to show that they can knock someone out with a slight strike to the area. However, this point is very dangerous and should never be used in demonstration. The point should be struck inward toward the back of the neck to cause instant knockout, death, or delayed death!

Antidote. If you have knocked someone out with a light touch, first squeeze in lightly at Gb 20; this should bring him around (then see a psychiatrist). What does not show is the delayed effect of stroke caused by the slow disintegration of the interior wall of the carotid artery.

Have an X ray taken every month for about six months to show any deterioration. The carotid sinus controls the blood pressure in the body. It is a baroreceptor, and when the blood pressure rises it causes the heart to slow, thus lowering the blood pressure. Cardiologists use this point to activate the carotid sinus and bring the blood pressure down, but only in extreme cases where death due to high blood pressure and extreme heart activity is imminent.

This is what Prof. Jim Lance, Australia's top neurologist, said when asked about the dangers of striking or "touching" the St 9 area (in an interview for an article published in *Fighting Arts* magazine and *Fighting Arts International*):

> **E.M.:** What about "just touching" the area to cause knockout—can that be done and why [or why not]?
> **P.L.:** Any doctor can do that to the carotid sinus to cause knockout with just a finger touch. I think that he's playing with fire, this chap.

. . . and this from the late Dr. Istvan Tork, professor of anatomy and physiology at the University of New South Wales (NSW):

> **E.M.:** Professor Tork, what are the implications of being touched or struck in the area of the carotid sinus?
> **P.T.:** Well, I would not like to be hit in that area, carotid or not. However, it depends upon what the person is doing in that area.
> For instance, it is used in cardiac medicine to not hit but push the carotid sinus when there is extreme high rate of heart function, and in order to reduce that one could apply pressure . . . but there is always the danger that the patient can black out—and that *is* dangerous. In those cases we would put the patient in the horizontal position until the blood pressure came back to normal again.

. . . and a very important word from Prof. James McCleod, head of cardiology at the Sydney University Medical Department:

> **E.M.:** Professor McCleod, what are the

medical implications of a slap to the carotid artery around the point we know as St 9, or the carotid sinus? Can it be done safely?

P.M.: Well, the answer is no, because you can actually rupture the carotid artery. I don't mean causing external bleeding, but you can tear the internal structure of it and get what is known as a dissection of it, which can result in a stroke. That's a well recognized diagnosis on the carotid artery.

E.M.: The artery is struck. It is struck in an inward manner towards the backbone.

P.M.: Yes, the trauma can damage the wall of it, so that internally it becomes split, and the internal part of the wall can break away and block the blood flow.

E.M.: I have asked one of our top acupuncturists about the carotid sinus, and he states that the reason people get knocked out is that the carotid sinus registers extreme high blood pressure when struck even lightly.

P.M.: That's right. When it is struck it registers high blood pressure when there really isn't high blood pressure, and then it causes the blood pressure to drop greatly, thus causing the person to faint. Normally it controls the blood pressure by increasing the blood pressure when the pressure inside the carotid sinus drops or, alternatively, when it goes up, reducing the blood pressure. So this is why they faint.

Stomach 15 and 16
Martial. Just over the pectoral muscle, St 15 and

16 will cause heart stoppage as a result of drainage when struck at a downward angle.

Antidote. Massage H 1 and H 3 and apply CPR if all else fails.

Martial. Striking these points at an upward angle will also cause heart stoppage, this time as a result of adding too much qi, which causes the heart to race.

Antidote. The antidote is the same as that used for a downward strike to these points.

Martial. When struck in a spiral, these points will cause complete loss of power in the lower body.

Antidote. Massage tan tien in both directions or Gb 21 straight in.

Stomach 15 and Gall Bladder 24

Martial. Striking these points across the body at the same time will cause knockout, instant heart stoppage, and death!

Antidote. There is no cure other than CPR.

Spleen 20

Martial. A straight-in strike to this point, on the front of the tip of the shoulder, takes out the use of that arm and can cause extreme liver failure.

Antidote. We push Liv 14 straight inward to bring the arm back. You could also use Liv 3.

Spleen 20 and Liver 14

Martial. Striking Sp 20 (6 cun lateral to the midline in the second intercostal space) and Liv 14 straight in with fingers will cause severe numbness of the body and paralysis in general. If done too hard it will cause the lungs and the heart to stop (fig. 64).

Antidote. There is no antidote.

Spleen 21 and Stomach 9

Martial. Striking Sp 21 (under the arms on the mid-axillary line in the sixth intercostal space) and St

9 straight in causes knockout as well as spleen damage and lung failure.

Antidote. Massage Sp 20 and 21 downward and grab the Gb 20s.

Triple Warmer 8
Martial. When struck straight in, Tw 8 will also cause the blood pressure to rise.

Antidote. Use Pc 6, pressing back toward the person's shoulder on the inside of the forearm.

Figure 64

Triple Warmer 17
Martial. Just behind the ears in the little concave, this is a death point when you strike your opponent from the back of his head toward you (when you are standing in front of him).

Antidote. There is no antidote.

Triple Warmer 23
Martial. When struck downward, this very useful dim-mak point located just over the outer corner of each eye will cause knockout by draining energy from the lower heating area.

Antidote. Push upward at Gb 20.

These are the major points that we in the World Taiji Boxing Association (WTBA) and the "Montaigue System" use. There are others, of course (and I will be covering more multiple strikes in the next chapters), but these are the ones I have found to be the easiest to execute—and the most dangerous.

CHAPTER FIVE

Multiple Strikes, Advanced Techniques, and Their Implications

The human body is really quite an amazing machine, with back-up systems in case of main failure, safety fuses, and auxiliary generators. If we know about human physiology, including acupuncture, then we are able to make use of this knowledge in our martial art. And that is exactly what the founders of many of the martial systems did way back when in China.

Many founders, especially those in the t'ai chi ch'uan and, indeed, all of the internal systems, would work with Chinese doctors and physiology experts in creating their arts of genius. In fact, the person to whom the invention of the original t'ai chi system is attributed, Chang Sung-feng, also founded dim-mak, that art which involves the striking of acupuncture points to cause grievous bodily harm. So every movement in the t'ai chi form, no

107

matter what style, is actually used for dim-mak.

After many years of training in a martial art, one must eventually ask the age-old question, "Is that all there is?" Many stay at the very basic stage of block, punch, kick, lock, and hold all of their lives. Others go on to more advanced and yet less complex methods, simultaneously blocking and attacking until the block becomes the attack and so on, and many can become quite excellent fighters in this way. But even this is not the highest level of dim-mak.

The highest level, in a martial sense, comes when you are able to actually put adverse energy into the points or drain energy from them, depending on what it is you are trying to achieve.

In this chapter I will cover some of the more advanced techniques, including multiple point strikes. By this I mean that we are able to use our block to actually strike to certain points in order to "set up" other, more deadly points, making them more vulnerable. As you study these techniques, bear in mind that all movement in dim-mak fighting must come from the waist and legs in a natural way. There must not be too much muscular force behind the fist, foot, or palm, etc., individually. The power must come from the movement of the body as a whole, and your muscles should be there only to control the direction of the attack.

In addition, I will include many techniques that enable us to get in and make use of the advanced point strikes. It's one thing to know the theory, but another to put it into practice.

Finally, we will look at something that is often left out of books such as this one—the implications of such strikes with regard to the human body and mind and the dangers thereof. As I have already said, you must be really sure that your life is in danger before embarking on a defense that will cause irreparable damage or death.

KNOCKOUT: WHY IT
HAPPENS AND HOW TO DO IT

It is possible to cause knockout by only striking the forearm, but such strikes have to be substantial to do so. Still, they are very dangerous, with even the lightest of slaps able to cause heart failure or death through carotid interior artery wall disintegration some weeks or months later. So please do not try it out; save it for a life-or-death situation and not just the big guy down at the pub who "kicks sand in your face." Let me explain.

There are a few ways that knockout can happen. The first way we all are aware of. In the event of a heavy strike to the head or face, the body causes us to black out so that more blood and oxygen are available to that sensitive and vital area.

Many of us also know about the old "choke out" hold, with which we are able to stop the flow of air to the lungs, thus causing the body to black out, the result being air blockage knockout (see fig. 65).

There are, however, easier ways to cause the lungs to contract violently, causing the person to think that he has received the proverbial kick in the guts. Striking certain points causes the muscles around the lungs to go into spasm, resulting in knockout. (Many of us have may have experienced this to a lesser degree when

Figure 65

we got up quickly one morning in the wrong way when perhaps we slept exposing our lower back area to the cold. All of a sudden we were struck with lung spasm which caused us to go down until the pain subsided and the lungs were no longer constricted.)

If we, for instance, block from the outside using what we in the internal arts call a hinge block, striking Colon 10 on the upper forearm (fig. 66), this opens up (makes vulnerable) the lung area. Then when we attack with the next strike, called slant flying in t'ai chi (fig. 67), aimed at stomach 16 and 17 points on the pectoral area, this causes the lungs to be constricted and so results in knockout. This technique can also be performed from the rear for the

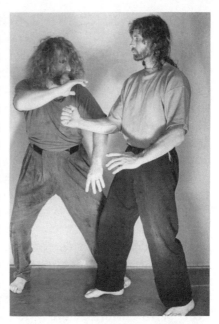

Figure 66

Figure 67

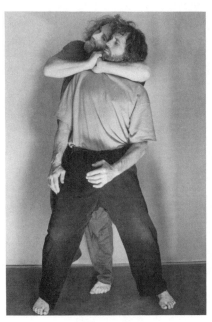

Figure 68

same effect, but this time we attack the point called Small Intestine 11, just in the center of the scapular.

A more complicated method of causing knockout, physiologically speaking, involves cutting off the blood supply to the brain, which brings results even sooner. If we just cause the head to turn slightly while applying the choke hold, we cause blockage knockout, as in Figure 68. The sleeper hold simply squeezes the carotid artery until the blood stops.

I am concerned when people do this technique in particular at seminars because it usually involves striking the carotid sinus.

The rest of this chapter will deal with the more advanced techniques of dim-mak. Here, I will be showing multiple strikes with set-up points. In order to use these techniques, it is important that one be well versed both in the material covered in the preceding chapters and in the fighting arts in general.

Advanced Point Technique #1

Your opponent attacks with straight right. In response, you aim for either Pericardium 6 (neigwan) or Heart 6. (Actually, you could be aiming at Heart 4, 5, 6, or 7, which are all close to each other in that area that's within one hand's grip back from the wrist.) An attack to either of these points, especially neigwan, drains energy from the body, taking away your opponent's will to continue. However, you *do*.

After successfully blocking the attack (fig. 69), you quickly step behind with the right foot and slam both of your palms downward with a twisting motion to attack the Gb 21 points on top of the shoulders (fig. 70). Striking the gall bladder points will cause the brain to lower the blood pressure greatly, thus resulting in knockout.

You can also stick the knee into bladder points on the back as you pull your opponent downward. The bladder points run along the length of the backbone on either side of it,

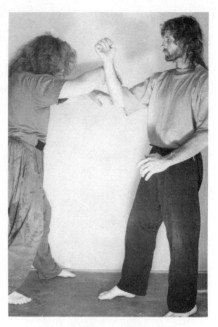

Figure 69

Figure 70

with the most potent ones being Bladder 16 and 17 (around the lungs and heart) and Bladder 22 and 23 (around the kidneys).

Alternatively, after the block you could have simply attacked Heart 6 and Lung 8 or 9 points on the inside and outside of the wrists by violently grabbing the wrists after the block and thrusting downward. This has the effect of either breaking or dislocating the neck, because attacking these two points simultaneously weakens it and makes it more vulnerable. It also causes the lung and heart energy to rush to those two points, leaving the rest of the body with much less qi and therefore weakened and vulnerable.

The Importance of the Wrists

This is an example of how vitally important the wrists are in dim-mak. Here we see every major organ in the body represented by points all clumped together within one hand's grab of the wristband. So any good twisting wrist lock will cause great damage, not only to the wrist but also to the internal organs the particular points represent.

The points represented on the wrist are: Lung 8 and 9; Heart 4, 5, 6, and 7; Small Intestine 5 and 6; Large Intestine 5; Pericardium 6 and 7; and Triple Warmer 4 and 5. So you do not have to know which points you are looking for, just how to grab the wrist for the greatest effect going against the flow of energy. This means that when you lock the wrist, you should do it so you are pushing the outside of the wrist in toward the body while pulling the inside of the wrist away from the body.

Look at the posture from pa-kua called "close the door and push the moon" (fig. 71). The basic meaning of this posture is that of a block and attack to the groin. But the inner meaning is a deadly block to wrist points, followed by a twisting wrist lock that pulls the energy in the wrong direction and also twists the wrist in toward the body, thrusting the opponent away (fig. 72). All wrist locks should be performed with this twisting motion against the flow of energy. Just a simple penetration punch to neigwan point on the inside of the wrist will put someone down and out before they are able to get anywhere near you.

Figure 71

So if you can block, you can attack! Your block must *become* your attack, because, as stated earlier, in dim-mak we are not just blocking but attacking vital points.

Another response to the initial straight right is to attack the Stomach 15 and 16 points. This time you block on the open side (i.e., block the opponent's left wrist, attacking the Pc 6 and H 6 points), and this time, be-

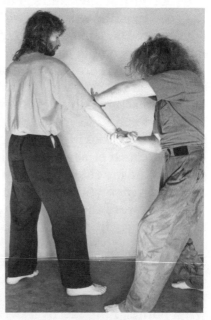

Figure 72

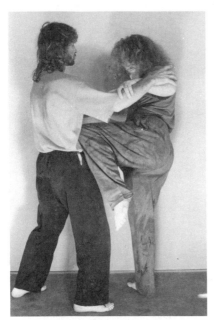

Figure 73

cause you are within range of his hands, you immediately step in closer and slam both palms down in a clockwise twisting motion onto his pectoral area, thus causing knockout. The wrist and St 15 and 16, when struck hard in combination, will cause the heart to stop.

You can also grab both wrists after the initial block, supposing your opponent has attacked with both hands, and jerk him downward onto the knee, thrusting into Gall Bladder 24 (fig. 73), a very dangerous point which will cause knockout and death when combined with the initial wrist point strikes.

You could have also used another gall bladder point, Gb 14. In this case, you can attack this point, which is centrally located just above the eyebrow,

Figure 74

with the side of the forehead as you jerk your opponent downward. When all four of these points (Gb 14, Gb 24, H 6, and Pc 6) are struck, death is imminent.

Advanced Point Technique #2

Block your opponent's right fist with your left palm from the outside, making sure that the strike is done in an outward, pushing way to upset the body energy. In other words, your left palm will rub his forearm back up his arm as it strikes. Your right palm simultaneously comes up underneath your left elbow, as in Figure 74. Simultaneously step to your left with your left foot and bring your right palm across to attack the Triple Warmer 17 point just behind the ear.

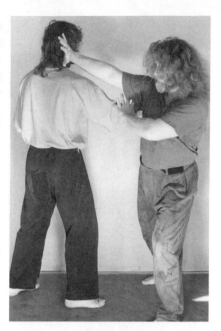

Figure 75

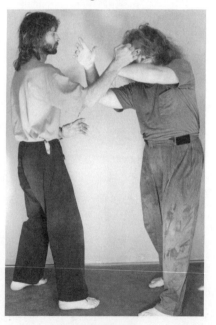

Figure 76

This technique causes death because the point is struck in exactly the right direction to stop the energy flow; that is, in a path heading in toward the front of the face from the neck. When combined with the initial set-up strike to the outside of the forearm, the effect is devastating (fig. 75).

Figure 77

Advanced Point Technique #3

Block your opponent's right palm with your left p'eng to Heart 4, 5, or 6, thus damaging his heart energy. Your right palm immediately and almost simultaneously comes over the top of your left palm (fig. 76) to take his right palm, swinging it over to your right as you swivel on your heels to your right and attack carotid sinus point St 9 with your left palm (fig. 77).

Advanced Point Technique #4 (Chee)

Known as a "chee" attack in taiji, this technique falls within a group of postures called "grasping swallow's tail" and is one of the "secret strikes."

Here, in response to your opponent's right lower rip, use the posture known as "roll back" to strike the inside of his right arm at Heart 3 and neigwan (fig. 78).

This set-up shot causes great weakness and energy drainage so that the dim-mak strike to Liv 14 (fig. 79) will have the optimum effect. The time between the two strikes is minimal—a split second and the body explodes into action using fa-jing. This combination will cause death, with little hope of revival.

Advanced Point Technique #5

Slam the inside of your opponent's low attacking left wrist (or both if he is attacking neigwan with both arms), as in Figure 80. This will, in itself, take all of the energy out of his lower body by attacking the diaphragm. Rotate both palms so they are facing up and spear his Liver 13 points on both sides with both hands (fig. 81). This, when used with the set-up point, will cause great damage to the internal organs. Now bring both elbows upward to attack Gall Bladder 24 points

Figure 78

Figure 79

Figure 80

Figure 81

on both sides (fig. 82) or Stomach 25, 26, 27, and 28, which run in a straight line down either side of the lower abdomen from the navel. Finally, turn both palms over and claw the eyes.

Advanced Point Technique #6

Block your opponent's attack with your left palm against his wrist points (mentioned earlier). Your right elbow now strikes his carotid sinus area, or Stomach 9 (fig. 83).

Now your right hammer fist can come back to strike the temple point (Gb 3) or other major points around the head. Or you can bring your right palm back, as in the other side of "fishes in 8" posture from taiji, to attack to his Stomach 9 points (fig. 84).

Advanced Point Technique #7

Shake your body from left to right in order to use your left palm to block your opponent's oncoming left attack, using the fingers of the right hand to strike Gb 1. The strike must go toward the face and use the tips of the fingers. This will cause dizziness and fainting on a small scale but will kill if great power is used (fig. 85).

Figure 82

Advanced Point Technique #8

Block your opponent's left attack with your right palm (fig. 86), then use the backs of both wrists to attack his Liv 13 points and come up in spirals (the left palm making a clockwise circle while the left palm makes a counterclockwise circle) to attack his St 15 and 16 points. This

Figure 83

Figure 84

Figure 85

combination caus-
es the liver to break
down, and then the
heart will stop.

**Advanced Point
Technique #9**

Turn to face an
attack from behind
and block your op-
ponent's left, slam-
ming your right
palm into his left Pc
6, thus draining his
energy. As both of
your palms roll
over, use the fingers
to attack Cv 14 and
Cv 4 (fig. 87). This
will first drain his
healing energy,
making the Cv
strike more danger-
ous. Break his right
arm by attacking
Tw 12 (fig. 88).
Attack St 9 and Liv
14 (fig. 89) and then
St 15 and 16 (fig. 90).

Alternatively,
use this same tech-
nique but finish by
attacking Cv 14
and K 16. First,
block his left from
the rear and then
attack the two
points. Striking K
16 by itself will

upset the balance of fire and water in the system, causing the person to feel really ill. Combining it with Cv 14 will cause complete disharmony in the body, causing joy and fear to join and make the person a mental wreck, as well as stopping the heart. There is no revival.

Advanced Point Technique #10

Block your opponent's left arm with your right hammer onto lung points on the top of his right wrist to affect the qi and weaken the body, as your left palm attacks Gv 26 under his nose (fig. 91).

Advanced Point Technique #11

Slam the Pc 6 point on the inside of your opponent's wrist after his low right attack to affect the qi, as

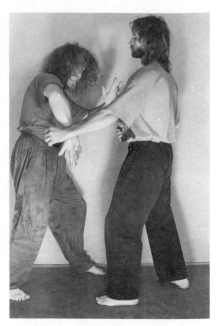

Figure 86

Figure 87

Figure 88

Figure 89

your right palm slams down onto Cv 17. This will severely drain the qi from his whole body and cause him to lose his seat of power.

Advanced Point Technique #12

Grab his straight right with your left palm, attacking the H 6 and L 5 points on his wrist in order to weaken him. This drains energy from the lungs. When used with neigwan, it is a body draining point. Then attack Sp 19 with the fingers of your right palm. This will weaken his legs greatly (fig. 92). Then pull his right palm down toward your knee as your right palm strikes his eyes or Gb 1, at the edge of the eye (fig. 93). This combination causes the whole body to go into spasm, and using the heart and lung points to set it up obstructs the free flow of qi throughout the body, as well as causing blindness by affecting the liver (which rules the eyes; the eyes turn yellow when the liver is affected).

Advanced Point Technique #13

Your opponent attacks with a straight right from the side. You turn and slam his Tw 9 with your left palm as the right backfist assists in locking the wrist (fig. 94). Your right palm now takes his wrist at the heart and lung points to weaken his body, while the palm of your left hand strikes Gb 3. This is a death point strike (fig. 95).

Advanced Point Technique #14

Attack the temple at Gb 3, using a penetration punch

Figure 90

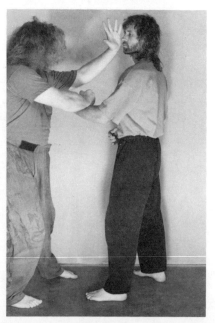

Figure 91

Figure 92

against your opponent's on-guard position or his straight left (fig. 96). Now use the backfist to attack Gb 14 (fig. 97). This combination of the two gall bladder points will cause knockout and eventually death as a result of the loss of qi to the heart.

Advanced Point Technique #15

Block your opponent's left attack with hinge and attack Cv 22 with your fingers (fig. 98). Barge into Gb 22 with your shoulder and bring a right slanting arm up under his armpit to attack H 1 (fig. 99).

This whole technique will cause death, with Cv 22 and Gb 22 working together to weaken the body. The final H 1 attack is the killer. It will also cause great psychological disorders when

Figure 93

used in combination with the heart and lung points on the wrist.

Advanced Point Technique #16

If you recall, striking St 3 upward will drain the lower heating area and make your opponent feel really sick. Set up by striking Tw 9 with your right palm, then rebound up and into St 3 (figs. 100 and 101).

Figure 94

Advanced Point Technique #17

In response to your opponent's initial strike, use either Pc 6 or Tw 9 as set-up points (fig. 102). Then, for the final blow, strike Tw 23 in a downward direction (fig. 103) to drain both the middle and lower heaters. (Tw 23 is used in healing to clear fire from the head, but if there is no fire in the head,

Figure 95

Figure 96

Figure 97

it drains the head completely, resulting in KO or death. Being struck here makes one really sick, taking the energy from the seat of power, the diaphragm.)

Advanced Point Technique #18

Swing around and block your opponent's right attack from the rear using your right palm (fig. 104). Swing his arm out with your right and attack the Liver 13 and 14 points with both palms (fig. 105). Note that the Liver 14 attack uses a centrifugal strike while the Liv 13 attack uses a pumping strike (left palm). Liver 13 promotes the spleen function of transformation and transportation of blood, etc., and relieves retention of food. When used by itself in a martial application, this point will cause diarrhea, vomiting, and spleen damage. Liver 14 will stop the qi flow, resulting in death. Put the two together and you have spleen knockout as well as liver knockout, also causing death.

DIM-MAK AND FA-JING AGAINST KICKS

Dim-mak can also be used to defend against kicks. Of course, when using the taiji system, we do not need to worry about kicks, as the technique of striking our opponent as soon as he comes within range applies to kicks as well, and therefore he never gets the chance to kick. However, as it is of interest to many people, I will discuss how to use the dim-mak points on the legs against various types of kicks.

Figure 98

Figure 99

Figure 100

Advanced Point Technique #19

High back kick. In response to this, we move in to show that all kicks are useless anyway, using eagle vision, barging, and so on. However, in Figure 106, he kicks and I step in and to the side, striking to the rear of the knee to K 10 or Bl 40. K 10 causes the qi to be drained from the lower heater when struck. It is also connected to Bl 40, which strengthens the waist when used for healing but, when struck, takes qi from the waist and causes knockout. Striking them together causes paralysis of the lower body.

Advanced Point Technique #20

Low back kick. Both Gb 33 and Gb 34 are knockout points. Striking them almost simultaneously causes the liver to become

Figure 101

too yin (weakened) and can cause death if hard enough (fig. 107).

Advanced Point Technique #21

High round-house. When your opponent kicks, simply move in and strike St 32, which causes the leg to become paralyzed.

Advanced Point Technique #22

Low round-house. Use the feet here and kick to Sp 8. When struck, Sp 8 causes qi drainage from the spleen and the person drops to the ground. Or kick Sp 9, which will drain the lower body of energy.

Advanced Point Technique #22

Low back kick. Kick Gb 34, which is a knockout point. Or kick Gb 35, which will cause the eyes to malfunction temporarily or, if the strike is hard, knockout.

Figure 102

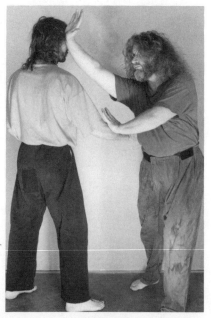

Figure 103

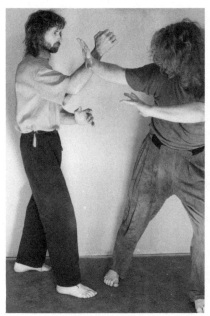

Figure 104

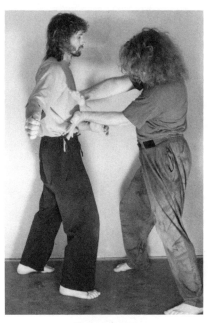

Figure 105

NEUROLOGICAL SHUTDOWN

This is a human phenomenon; it does not happen to animals. When we are struck in a certain way to certain parts of the face, the whole nervous system shuts down and we faint. These techniques are excellent for use by women or smaller people, as all they have to do is slap in the right areas to cause KO. There are two parts of the face which, when struck in a certain way, will cause neurological shutdown.

Advanced Point Technique #23

The first encompasses points above the eye and under the cheekbone, and these must be struck simultaneously. So the back of the palm is an ideal weapon to strike this area, as shown in Figure 108. The attack

Figure 106

Figure 107

Figure 108

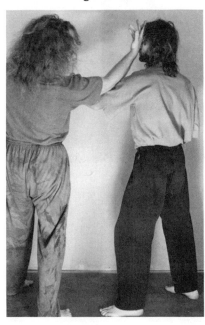

Figure 109

must be a whipping motion and not a push, or shutdown will not occur (fig. 109). The points must be slapped.

Advanced Point Technique #24

The second is the whole jaw area. If you place your middle finger of your right palm just under the jawbone with the largest knuckle lying across Si 17 and then close your fingers, you will see the exact area. Again, slap this area with a whipping motion.

COMBINED NEUROLOGICAL, DIM-MAK, AND NERVE POINT STRIKES

There are hundreds of these strikes and combinations, so to give you an idea of how to look for them and how to combine them, I will include one here taken directly from taiji.

Advanced Point Technique #25

Your opponent attacks with a right hook. You slam it with the back of your right palm into the crease of his right elbow, causing great nerve damage (fig. 110). Notice where the left palm is. It is already coming up and under your right forearm to strike, using "tiger paw fist," the knuckle of the middle finger, straight into H 3, causing the heart to falter (fig. 111) This is the dim-mak part. You finish off with the neurological strike across the eye and cheekbone, using the back of the hand, as in Figure 112. This whole process takes only a split second to execute.

Figure 110

Figure 111

Figure 112

WILLOCKS BROS. CO., INC.

1021 Foch Street
MARYVILLE, TENNESSEE

Maryville Ph. 983-3971   Knoxville Ph. 637-1631

Lovell Rd. Ph. 966-0875

490

CHAPTER SIX

Secret Circular Hand Techniques

These twelve techniques are indeed the most dangerous ever invented. They make use of the most deadly dim-mak strikes and combinations. Back in the days when our lives depended upon our hands, a martial artist who had reached the most advanced levels of taiji would be given one of these techniques per year for 12 years, and only when he had proven himself to be a master of his art, his technique, and, more importantly, himself.

These techniques come directly from the founders of dim-mak (taiji) and are based upon continuing circular movements of the hands totally coordinated with the footwork and fa-jing. These techniques are the culmination of all that one has learned in dim-mak.

We first of all practice them using mitts, with a partner holding two mitts at the appropriate places to represent the points on the body which we will be striking. Once we have learned one technique, we practice it until we are able to execute it on the count of one (i.e., as quickly as possible without losing power, technique, or accuracy). Then we have our partner attack us in a specific manner so that we are able to practice on an actual person (pulling our attacks, of course). Then we have our partner use random attacks (e.g., with two arms, one fist, etc.).

Note: With each of the strikes below, the other "controlling" hand also strikes, usually the forearm, to set up the points each time. You borrow the movement from fa-jing to do this, so it requires no more use of energy; it just happens. That's the beauty of fa-jing—the whole body must do it (or it isn't fa-jing), so you just place your palm, elbow, knee, or whatever at the correct point and allow it to do the work for you.

Circular Hand Technique #1

Your partner holds the two mitts about 2 feet apart and about head level. You first strike his right-hand mitt with the dim-mak "curved but straight" snap punch from a very short distance, with the fist closing only upon impact, like a whip cracking (fig. 113).

Now the fist will roll over coun-

Figure 113

Figure 114

Figure 115

terclockwise to strike his left-hand mitt with the "dog punch." I have not found this punch in any other martial art, and it is quite devastating when used to the correct parts of the body.

The fist makes contact as shown in Figure 114 and uses the last three knuckles, as does the first punch. Your partner should feel great power as you strike.

Now you do it against your partner's attack, in this case a right straight. You do not even block his attack, but rather, using eagle vision, move slightly as soon as he moves to your right, avoiding his attack. You have already taken his face off by striking Gv 26 (fig. 115).

That fist immediately circles into a "dog" fist to the neck area at Si 16 (fig. 116), and as you move to his left you strike his carotid sinus area (St 9) with the "bat falls to earth" palm as the counterclockwise twisting left palm pounds his lower abdomen at Gb 24 (fig. 117). This whole technique has only taken a split second. You have struck at four major dim-mak points before he knows what is happening.

You then do it on the other side, and while you are moving your partner takes a step back and throws his left fist at you. You also take one step forward and perform the whole technique on the left side. You can move up and down the room doing this technique.

Figure 116

Circular Hand Technique #2

Again, the technique is first used on the mitt and then you do it with a partner.

He attacks again with any kind of attack, and you barge into Stomach 9 with your left fingers using "drilling palm" as your right palm attacks Gb 24 (fig. 118). Then this

Figure 117

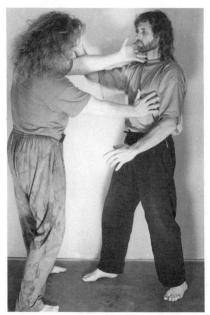

Figure 118

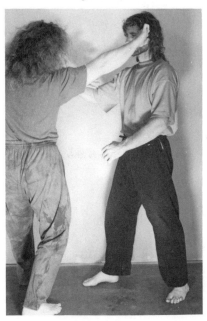

Figure 119

power is redirected into a right penetration punch to the temple area (Gb 3) as the left palm also uses the power from fa-jing to attack the inside of his right arm in a negative qi flow direction, toward you (fig. 119).

You *must* make use of this rebound and keep the fa-jing going. The right fist immediately flows into a backfist as you do a change step (bringing the front foot back and rear foot forward) into Cv 24 (fig. 120) and then direct a "sideways turning palm"—a slap with the right palm, thumb upward—to Si 17 (fig. 121).

Circular Hand Technique #3

This next method involves only the palms. Again, your opponent attacks with any sort of attack. In this example, he will use his right straight. So you again barge in with a simultaneous strike to the inside of his right forearm to set up the whole technique using your left palm.

Remember, by this time you have progressed so far that the set-up points have become ingrained in your subconscious, so it does not matter what attack is launched, you just react with the correct set-up point. However, it is usually against the inside or outside of the forearms, either against or with the flow of energy, depending upon what kind of second and main attacks you have planned.

The right palm is an eagle claw to the eyes. The eyes are also a dim-mak striking point, of course, and a most devastating one. All you need to do

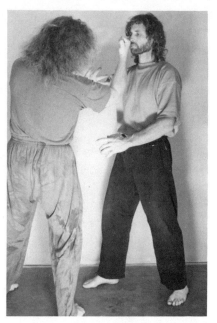

Figure 120

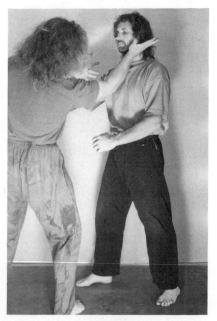

Figure 121

Figure 122

Figure 123

is lightly scrape your fingers across the eyeballs and the fight is finished (fig. 122).

This eagle claw rolls into a back palm across the neurological shutdown points on the upper eye and cheekbone (fig. 123) and then into the "nun offers food" palm to the chin, pushing it backward while the fingers of the right palm dig into Cv 22. The right palm then takes hold of anything that it can and drags it while the left palm again attacks the face. There has also been a foot change for this last part (fig. 124).

Remember that these parts of the whole technique only take a second to execute. People often say to me that the attacker would be finished after the first part anyway. Yes, this what is known as the art of over-kill—just to be sure.

Circular Hand Technique #4

Your right palm pounds across and cuts the attacker's right arm at the elbow as you step across him to your left (fig. 125). This is a nerve strike and severely damages the whole nervous system, to say nothing of what it does to the arm.

Your left palm then snakes upward and across his eyes to claw him backwards (fig. 126), and your right pounding palm crashes across his neck at Cv 22 as he falls (fig. 127).

Circular Hand Technique #5

Use "sit back ready" (from the main taiji form) to jab your opponent's eyes (or St 3 in an upward direction) and simultaneously block his attack and strike the set-up points on the inside of his

Figure 124

Figure 125

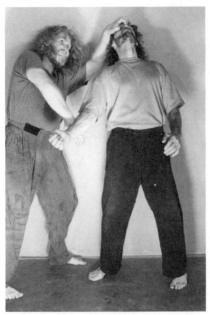

Figure 126

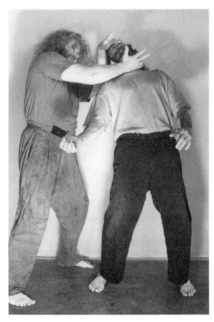

Figure 127

right forearm. You are in a natural right stance now (fig. 128).

Turn the finger jabs into a tiger paw fist facing upward to attack Gv 26 under his nose (fig. 129). Turn the right palm over and attack his Gb 14 with a downward strike to further drain energy, and change step as you do this to the side (fig. 130).

Attack his face, striking the "mind point" from front to rear and slightly inward with a left palm as you grab his left arm as in the third technique (fig. 131). Then follow with a reverse elbow to his Gb 24 points in the lower rib area (fig. 132).

Circular Hand Technique #6

Again attack and block with snake fingers in a natural stance, as in the previous technique. Take your opponent's left arm with your right palm as your left palm pounds into the right side of his face at the mind point (fig. 133).

Now the snake fingers of your right palm again attack his St 9 and the thumb strikes Cv 22 (fig. 134). Now the right palm takes the back of his neck, and as you change the step, pull his neck forward as your left palm attacks the forehead at Gb 14 in an upward way, thus breaking the neck (fig. 135).

Circular Hand Technique #7

Slam the outside of your opponent's forearm at Tw 9 with your right fist as he attacks with his right fist (fig. 136). Your right fist immediately grabs his right arm, and

Figure 128

Figure 129

Figure 130

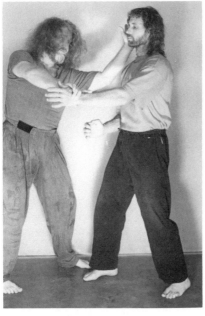

Figure 131

your left palm strikes just above his elbow to Tw 11 (fig. 137). This combination completely drains energy from the whole body, and it could break his arm at the elbow.

Your left palm now keeps his right arm still as your right palm attacks his neck on the left side at St 9 using "knife edge palm" (fig. 138). Next, your right palm reaches around the back of his neck and pulls it forward as your left knife edge cuts upward into the neck at Cv 23 (fig. 139). Then your left palm pulls him forward from the back as your right palm attacks his St 9 points again (fig. 140).

Circular Hand Technique #8

Slam your opponent's right attack with the back of your right palm into the crease of his elbow. This is a nerve strike (fig. 141).

Now, with the back of the same palm, slam his left arm as it attacks, as you jab to his eyes with the fingers of your left hand (fig. 142). Hook your right palm over his left elbow and lift the elbow upward, locking his left palm under your arm, thus breaking his arm. (fig. 143). Snake your left palm under his left palm and lift it upward as your right hammer fist slams into his Gb 24 or Liv 13 points in the lower rib area (fig. 144).

Figure 132

Circular Hand Technique #9

Take your opponent's attack with two palms, fingers downward and pointing toward him (spear fingers), open side or closed side. Jab into the pit of his neck at Cv 22 (fig.

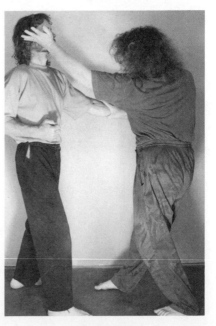

Figure 133

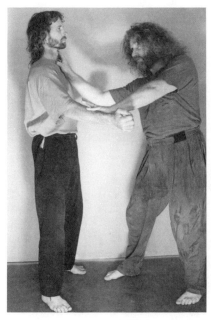

Figure 134

Figure 135

145). Now force his head backward by striking under his chin with the backs of both palms using fa-jing (fig. 146). Now slam both palms down into his St 9 points on both sides. Then push his head over to your right with your left palm as your right palm snakes over the top of your left palm and around the back of his neck. Now push his head upward, exposing his neck, and cut down across the neck with the knife edge of your left palm (fig. 147).

Circular Hand Technique #10

This is the same as for the first technique, with the punch to the face. Your right strikes your opponent's mind point (fig. 148). Your left palm snakes across the left side of his neck, grabbing it from the back and pul-

ling his head for-
ward onto your
right tiger paw at
Cv 22 (fig. 149).
Now your left palm
slams into his face
at the mind point
as your right palm
snakes under it,
grabbing his neck
again to drag him
forward onto your
right knee as the
left palm slams
into Si 11 and the
knee attacks Gb 24
(fig. 150).

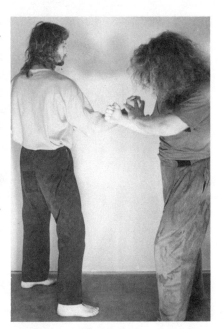

Figure 136

Circular Hand
Technique #11

Slam your oppo-
nent's right arm at
the elbow to block
and to cause ner-
vous damage. Your
left fingers attack
Cv 22 (fig. 151).
Bring the right
palm up into his
face, using the back
of the palm to
strike Gv 26 in an
upward way, as the
left palm controls
that same arm (fig.
152). Claw down
into his eye sock-
ets in a downward
way using the right

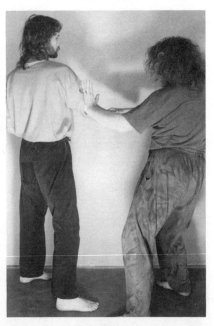

Figure 137

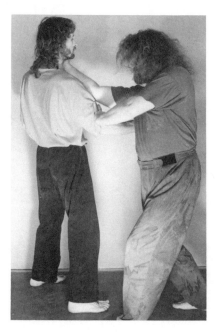

Figure 138

Figure 139

palm (fig. 153). That palm takes over his initial attacking hand as your left elbow comes across to strike his neck at Si 16 (fig. 154).

Circular Hand Technique #12

This attack is the same as the first technique, using the fist. Bring that fist back for a lateral attack to your opponent's carotid sinus as the left palm attacks his Gb 1 point at the edge of his right eye (fig. 155). Then bring both fists and palms back again to attack laterally in the other direction to the same points on his opposite side (fig. 156). Then attack the neck straight into Cv 22 with both tiger fists, using a slightly inward thrust so that they would meet each other if they kept going (fig. 157). Now grab the back of the neck with both palms and jerk it forward and out to the side to break it, and then come back with hinge elbow to the neck (fig. 158).

* * * * *

Some people look at these techniques and say "ugh!" But I stress again that these techniques are so dangerous that they would probably never be used. Only in the most dire situation should they even be thought of. However, they are good to do just as a solo training method, as they are completely circular and the energy from one leads nicely into the other. These are the epitome of what taiji (dim-mak) is all about.

Figure 140

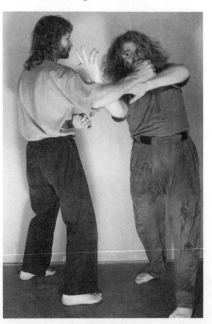

Figure 141

Figure 142

Figure 143

Figure 144

Figure 145

Figure 146

Figure 147

Figure 148

Figure 149

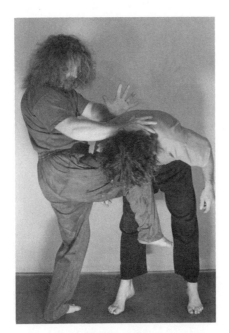

Figure 150

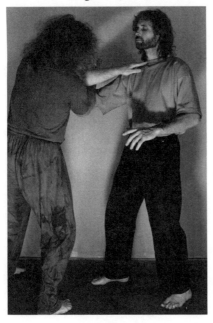

Figure 151

SECRET CIRCULAR HAND TECHNIQUES   157

Figure 152

Figure 153

158   DIM-MAK: DEATH-POINT STRIKING

Figure 154

Figure 155

Figure 156

Figure 157

Figure 158

CHAPTER SEVEN

The Healing Art of Dim-Mak

The healing art associated with dim-mak is probably the highest level that anyone can aspire to. At this level, you have taken in all that there is to know about the fighting art and you are using it to heal people, not to kill.

Usually, when people come to me for training (and I might add here that I only take on students nowadays who are willing to stick it out on an individual basis, one on one—I no longer teach beginner's classes, as I have done my 20 or so years of that), they come for the fighting aspects. They want to know how to defend themselves in the easiest and deadliest way.

Men, in particular, seem to be unsure of themselves, and I guess this goes back to the times when we literally had to fight for our lives. I don't have this problem with women; they seem to have a much more together attitude than the men. Deep within, men have this uncertainty: "Could I really defend my wife and kids if they were ever attacked?" And so with men, we first have to jump that hurdle. After only three or four months of using the methods contained in this book, the men usually realize that they *are* able to defend themselves. Then we can get down to learning the whole system correctly.

With the men, the desire to fight has gone after a few years; they know they don't even need to think about it any more—it's too basic. By this time they have usually moved on to the more important aspects, the healing. When we get to be over 40 years old, we usually want to look at the healing aspects, not only for ourselves, but so we know how to heal others.

In order to heal anyone else, you must also have a reserve of qi to give to others. Obviously, if your own reserves are low, then you will drain qi from those you are trying to heal. I have actually seen acupuncturists put needles into people with a fag hanging out of their mouths. Or others who are so sick themselves that their patients leave sicker than when they arrived!

QIGONG
What I have not yet covered in this book (as it would end up being like a set of encyclopaedias) is the "qigong." This is where we learn how to first heal ourselves at the very beginnings of our training. And usually, this exercise really weeds out the men from the boys (that is, those who come to learn only for ego or other reasons, in order to hurt someone; usually by the end of the first qigong session, that sort leaves and never returns because he realizes it is too hard and can't take it). The ones who stay go on to greater heights and learn the whole system.

The qigong allows us to heal ourselves and others by putting in the healing qi. It's the same initial qi as for dim-mak, but now it is used in a positive way, to heal. One of my students, a night watchman, was having a nice chat and a cup of tea with one of his associates at one of the better hotels where he was looking after the car park. In crashed two hooded gunmen with shotguns. Now this man is only a recent student of mine, but he is already well versed in self-defense, as he has studied wing chun for many years and teaches at his own school. However, there was absolutely nothing he could do here. The gunmen were about 12 feet away and were about to murder him if he so much as moved!

The reality of the situation was instant—he knew that he could not do a damn thing (and rightly so, as he is married with kids and so does not wish to be blown away!). The gunmen hog-tied him with gaffer tape—ears, eyes, and mouth as well—and proceeded to beat the living daylights out of the older man who was the watchman of the whole hotel until he told them the combination of the safe. They then shot him through the stomach anyway. In the meantime, my student had the strength—after having several ribs broken with the barrel of the shotgun—to slide his body backward, thus lifting his two-way radio out of its holster. With his nose pressing the button, he was able to call in his security code and summon help. Later, he told me that it was the qigong that was the most useful to him at that time. It stopped him from going into shock and allowed him to react in the correct way for that situation—calm and easy going, even when they were breaking his ribs. He said afterward that he hardly felt the ribs being broken.

So I tell people that the martial arts nowadays are used to help you on a broader level than just self-defense. The martial arts are excellent for their aesthetic value and because they are very interesting and because the healing aspects are great. But with modern weapons so easy to come by now, our martial arts sort of become redundant.

One of the best martial arts is simply to avoid being in the wrong places. It's a sorry old world, I know, but that's the way of it and we just have to live with it. There was a time when there was some sort of twisted honor among thieves, where, in the above case, for example, the thieves would not have beaten the old chap but rather slipped him a few hundred for his trouble and let him be. But nowadays, with the insurgence of drugs, there is no honor.

So now that I have caused you to feel really great, on with the qigong!

To some people this word "qigong" means magical, mystical feats of superhuman strength, such as old men bending iron bars in their nostrils or breaking granite blocks with their heads. To others it means a way of healing certain diseases otherwise incurable using Western medicine. To others it's a new fitness or exercise fad.

Many external stylists are now turning their attention back to their roots and the Chinese systems, namely qigong, to enhance their arts. Many are finding that they are only able to take their art to a certain high level, at which point their bodies just won't do any more. That's when they turn to qigong.

Some karate styles have tried to invent their own qigong systems, and some have been successful, but others have taken their qigong to the same absolute tension that their katas have to be taken and so have failed at gaining that something extra from their arts.

So what is qigong? Well it's not a way of becoming superman, so those who are considering taking it up to make them invincible can forget it. However, if you want to learn how to use what you have more economically and with much more natural power, and in the process become extremely well, then qigong is for you. You will not be able to perform such feats as the old spear-in-the-neck trick. This is a trick of leverage, wherein the attacker actually handles the spear so that the power is going upward onto the chin and not into the neck.

You don't have to be studying a Chinese style to use qigong. All that is required, especially for the "hard" stylists, is that you completely open up to a new way of doing things which will, in the beginning, be totally alien to what you have been taught.

Qigong allows your natural internal energy (electricity) to flow freely to all parts of the body. There are 12 main and eight extra acupuncture meridians throughout everyone's body. These are the channels for the flow of qi, and some of them *are* in your head! So you will not go mad from the practice of qigong if the qi gets into your brain, for God's sake! It *has* to. As we grow older and we become more tense (usually as a result of twentieth-century living), these channels are gradually blocked to the flow of qi until they become completely blocked and we die of something that the doctors put down to some disease that has attacked us from the outside. More to the point, the qi has slowed down to the point of stopping our natural self-healing mechanism from working correctly.

In the martial arts we use qigong not only to make us well, but also to give us something else in the way of power and speed. Obviously, if our muscles are so tense from overdoing weight training, we are unable to use them correctly. We sometimes use our muscle groups adversely so that different groups work against each other. This muscular tension then stops the bones, tendons, and sinews from working correctly and our whole body becomes rigid, usually to the point of putting bones permanently out of place. As a result, we can only make use of, for instance, the triceps muscles when throwing a punch, rather than using the whole body to whip the punch out at great speed and power. You can have big muscles, but they must not become so tight that they are always active when they should not be.

There are about 2,000 different types of qigong, grouped into three main areas, as follows:

Self-healing. This is where we are able to use certain postures with certain deep breathing techniques to allow our own self-healing mechanism to spring back to life, sending life-giving qi to all parts of the body via the meridians.

Medical. This is where we are able to heal others who are sick by putting in our own qi into their acupuncture points to assist their healing system. This is, however, quite advanced and takes years to master. We use certain breathing techniques with certain yin and yang palm postures to send a continuous flow of energy into the point. An acupuncture point is simply a point on the animal body at which there is a minimal amount of resistance to electrical energy. A seasoned practitioner can pick up these points by simply rubbing his palms gently over the patient's body until there is a slight "dragging or sticking" feeling, which indicates where they are situated. Only the point that needs the healing will be sticky, though, and this is where qigong is far more advanced than acupuncture.

Martial Arts. This is where we use certain postures with breathing techniques to cause a flow of qi to particular groups of muscles to help them work more effectively and with much more power. However, everyone must begin with the basic qigong for good overall health. First we must build up some more of this stuff called qi. For this we have a stance called "3 circle standing qigong."

First Hand Posture

Stand as shown in Figure 159. The knees are bent slightly so that the kneecaps are lined up vertically with the tips of the second toes. The buttocks must be tucked under slightly so that there is no sway in the lower back, but don't tuck under too much, as this will cause tension. The toes are curled under so that the middle of the foot is concave. The whole back must be vertical to the ground; look into a mirror at your side to check this. The chin must be pulled in lightly, with the tip of the tongue pressed lightly onto the hard palate where the tooth ridge begins (like you are saying "L").

The eyes must look down at an angle so that your gaze is focused about 20 feet away. The breathing must be in and out through the nose. The palms are positioned as if you are holding onto a large tree. Notice that there is a straight line of skin between the thumb and forefinger; this keeps the "circle" in

Figure 159

the palm and activates the point called "dragon mouth point," or Colon 4. The elbows are hanging slightly and are not lifted. If a slight swaying to and fro occurs naturally, then let it happen; this is all part of it. There will be a slight tremor coming up from the ground through your whole body, causing you to shake. This is because the qi finds an easy path down to the point just under your feet between the two toe mounts called Kidney 1 or "bubbling well point," but it has difficulty getting back up because of tension; thus the shake, like a wave hitting a wall. Once you have been standing in this posture for at least 15 minutes twice per day (morning and night) for about five weeks, this shaking becomes a mild vibration which is not at all unpleasant. There is a slight lifting of the anus sphincter internally (not tense) on the in breath and a releasing on the out breath, but this must not be taken to extremes, and no tension must be felt in the lower abdomen, as this could cause hernia if done too hard.

You must hold this first position for two-thirds of the total time. So if you intend to hold a total of 15 minutes, you will hold the first posture for 10 minutes and the next for the remaining five minutes.

Second Hand Posture

Without losing the "no mind" that you have gained, slowly lower your palms, so that they are at the level shown in Figure 160. Note that the elbows have not come in, but rather, there is a distance about the circumference of a tennis ball under your arms. You hold this posture for one-third of the total time and then

Figure 160

Figure 161

Figure 162

begin the "getting out" postures.

Finishing
Slowly allow your palms to float upward as you breathe in (fig. 161). Bring the palms across in front of you, as in Figure 162, and push downward with an out breath as you straighten your legs back to the normal standing position.

Breathing
There are four main breathing techniques that we must use with qigong. Here I will only deal with the first, as it takes three years of practice before going on to each successive technique. They are: natural breath, reverse breath, prenatal breath, and tortoise breath.

Natural Breath
This breathing technique is as it sounds, but the breathing of most

people has become unnatural, so we must first learn how to breathe naturally again. Look at a small child before any "living stress" has entered his or her mind. Children breathe with the lower part of their abdomens, where the bulk of the lungs is. Most people tend to breathe only with the upper portion of the lungs, drawing in their abdomens and sticking out their chests. If you simply relax your whole upper body (shoulders, chest, etc.), then there is only one way that you are able to breathe: stick out your gut on the in breath and allow it to collapse on the out breath, like a balloon filling up and deflating. Don't force your breath, just allow your motor reactions to work for you. Breathe in and out when you want to, and only breathe in until your lungs are full; don't try and get more air in there.

This is the natural way of qigong breathing, and when combined with the stances, it makes for a most potent healing/martial aid.

Martial Stances

I can't, of course, cover all of the qigong stances here, so I will cover one of the more useful ones for the martial arts.

Once you have trained in the healing qigong for at least three months and you are able to hold the stance for at least 20 minutes, then you should go on to the more strenuous martial qigong stances.

Holding the Baby

The normal healing qigong takes an equal amount of qi to the upper and lower body, while the martial qigong is able to take different amounts of qi to different parts of the body, depending upon which parts need it most. Most martial artists need much support from their legs, so we begin with the legs. The "holding the baby" qigong looks just like the name implies, as seen in Figure 163. You are now standing with most of your weight on one leg or the other (right leg in the photo),

Figure 163

with the palms held so that the elbows are over the corresponding knees. This puts the leading palm out further than the rear palm. As in the second hand posture, the one line of skin between thumb and forefinger is held, and the breathing is the same. The gaze must be out over your "dragon mouth point." The inner palm is placed 7 cun from the other wrist. (In Chinese measurement, from the wrist to the elbow is 12 cun.) The body is held in the same manner as for 3 circle standing qigong, only now you must notice what is referred to in the Chinese translation as "the three things."

It is important to take note of three areas of this stance, otherwise you could do yourself some damage—your muscles could collapse! First there will be a piercing pain, like a red-hot needle gong into your standing thigh. Next you will feel this pain dissipate all over your thigh, and then you will begin to shake. This is the time to change to the other leg. Don't just stop and change legs, though. Slowly shift your weight onto your left leg (other leg), and bring your right palm (inner palm) under your left palm. Take a step with your right foot so that you end up in the opposite position of the one you started in.

You now repeat the "three things" and then change back to the other leg. You will notice that each time you change you are able to hold the posture longer. You should be able to get it up to about three minutes, but not all at once. Make sure that you give each leg the same amount of time.

USING DIM-MAK POINTS FOR HEALING

Again, if we know what the dim-mak points do in the fighting art, we can also use them for healing. For instance, when Gb 14 is struck in an upward way, the effects are the same as a severe case of sunstroke. The exact same antidote that we use for the martial strike can be used to heal sunstroke. The revival points of Gv 26, Gv 20, Gb 20 and 21, etc., can be used not only for the martial arts but for anyone who has been injured or knocked out.

I will include a brief section here on using dimmak points to help yourself throughout the day. These same points are used to revive and as antidote points. If, for instance, someone has been struck so that the qi to the head has been drained, you will know the correct points to use to take the yang qi back to the head.

Before Going to Bed or in the Early Morning

You are lying in bed and just can't get to sleep, probably because of too much colon activity.

Daily Healing Technique #1

Lie on your back and place the palms under the lower back so that the backbone is across the wrists. Put pressure onto the wrists. This activates the whole wrist area: Co 5 (on the right wrist, it's in the hollow on the right side of the back of the wrist), Si 5 (on the other side of the same wrist in the hollow over on the side), and Tw 4 (back toward the middle of the right wrist but still to the left in the hollow on the wristband).

Co 5 draws qi down from the fire to make lower heater more active and increase the movement of fluids, especially if slowed by cold.

Tw 4 relaxes the tendons (nerves), reinforces the three heaters, strengthens jung (chong) mei (lifeline) and ren mei (conceptor vessel), removes heat (so you can sleep), and stimulates the qi in the meridians. It strengthens the overall communication between the three heaters and cools and nourishes the blood. The heart and liver are strengthened as well.

Si 5 is the fire and jing (qi in purified form) point, used to treat fever, deafness, tinnitus, and yang madness. If you have weakness due to blockages within the small intestine, such as "damp obstruction," the weakness causes a backlog of qi and fluid in the stomach (blocking digestion) and gall bladder. This is due to the physical connection of the small intestine to the stomach and gall bladder through the common bile duct. Activating this point increases circulation through the small intestine and relieves the blockages.

Daily Healing Technique #2

Close the fists and put pressure onto the lower back on either side of the backbone at Bladder 23, 24, and 25.

Bl 23 (1.5 cun lateral to the backbone on either side of the second lumbar vertebra) regulates and strengthens the kidneys. It is used for menstrual pain and all disorders of the kidneys. It makes the kidneys more yang to enhance their performance and is used for tonification and regulation of the whole system. It especially benefits the lower heater, which is controlled by the kidneys. It helps the kidneys to produce wei qi (the energy that flows over the whole body via the skin, used to protect us from disease), so the whole body's defenses will benefit.

Bl 24 (1.5 cun lateral to the third lumbar vertebra) increases the circulation of qi in the lower heater, where things are stored for later use (pot belly or fat thighs), bringing stored qi back into use. It is good, therefore, for fat people to lose weight in these areas.

Bl 25 (1.5 cun lateral to the fourth lumbar vertebra) acts upon the colon and the lower back and regulates the stomach qi. It is used to relieve constipa-
tion, diarrhea, and abdominal distension. It helps in
the production of wei qi.

Daily Healing Technique #3

Press St 3 upward while pressing Lu 3 and 4
straight in. St 3, just under the eye in the ridge, activates the stomach qi. Lu 3, 3 cun below the anterior
axillary fold, just outside the biceps, controls the
balance of qi between the body and head. It is used
for emotional and mental disorders, such as the
inability to cry or let go, and helps to disperse harmful emotions. When Lu 3 is used with Lu 4, 1 cun
below it, look out! This is a combination that activates the sexual energy, increasing the libido.

Press all three points simultaneously by using
your right fingers to activate the lung points on the
left arm while your left fingers activate St 3.

Daily Healing Technique #4

Squeeze the right wrist, then rotate it in toward
you in a counterclockwise direction. This helps to
clear the colon. Carry on up the forearm in this
manner on both arms.

Daily Healing Technique #5

Press Gb 35, at the back of the leg, just to the
right of center, on the outside of the fibula. This
activates the elimination process.

Daily Healing Technique #6

Open your hips and lie there on your belly on
the left side of your bed. Drop your right knee over
the edge of the bed and press your pelvis down on
to the bed. This, too, helps to activate the elimination process and is good for a sore back and lower
back problems.

First Thing after Rising (Perhaps in the Shower)
Daily Healing Technique #7

Upon rising in the morning, cross your wrists, right over left, in front of your chest. Press inward with both hands at the point where your middle finger reaches, which is Lu 1. (Lu 2 is just under the clavicle in the middle of it. Lu 1 is 1.2 cun below that.) This mobilizes and circulates the qi, as well as balancing the qi in the lungs and spleen. It will literally "get you going" for the day.

Daily Healing Technique #8

Press Cv 14 (just over the xiphoid process and 7 cun superior to the navel on the midline) for a general calming effect. This calms the mind, pacifies the stomach, and balances the qi. It serves to clear the upper heater and thus calms the heart and shen (spirit).

Daily Healing Technique #9

Press Cv 24, in the hollow of the chin, straight inward and slightly downward. This will regulate the qi throughout the body and maintain a proper balance of qi. Now that you are awake and going for it, you need the colon to quiet down; this point does this, harmonizing the stomach and the colon qi, so you are ready to take on the day.

Daily Healing Technique #10

You have an important meeting or job interview, so you press Gv 26, just under the nose, straight inward. It calms the mind and relaxes the whole body, especially if used with H 7 (shen men, or doorway to the spirit). Squeezing H 7, in the hole on the wrist crease, calms the shen and restores its emotional control over the whole system. This point is often used in conjunction with H 3 for emotional problems and insomnia.

Up and Going: Middle of the Day or Full Yang

Now you need the full yang energy at your disposal so that you can complete your daily tasks with the greatest amount of qi available to you.

Daily Healing Technique #11

To get the circulation going, press Lu 9, on the outer edge of the wrist just over that big tendon in the hollow, between radius and scaphoid. Because this regulates and strengthens lungs, it is used for yin disorders of the lungs. It also regulates respiration and is used for asthma, cough, sore throat, epistaxis, and migraine. It clears upper heater blockages and regulates the pericardium/heart, helping to control heart palpitations and the circulation of blood in general. It is good for skin conditions because of its actions on the liver and kidneys.

Daily Healing Technique #12

Apply pressure with your thumb to activate Co 1, on the outer edge of the index finger, just under the base of the fingernail. This circulates the liver qi and gives us strength in the limbs (among other things). It is also good for toothaches. When the yang energy has reached its peak, activating this point will provide a boost so that you can get a little more out of your qi.

Daily Healing Technique #13

Squeeze Co 2, in the depression of the first knuckle of the index finger. This is another good point for moving the bowels. It regulates the balance of fluid within the colon and promotes its assimilation to the kidneys. It also regulates the yin/yang balance and moves the qi to nourish the yang.

Daily Healing Technique #14

Press St 17, at the center of the nipple, straight in, with a slight upward motion. This stimulates the middle heater (digestion), as well as the production of blood or, in nursing mothers, milk.

Daily Healing Technique #15

Press H 3 (just in the crease of the inner elbow, about 1 cun from the elbow inward and back about 5 fen toward the shoulder) to help with tension, emotional stress, and depression. So when your day has not been too good, use this point to keep you going and prevent stresses from affecting you too badly. It calms the heart fire and pacifies the *shen*, as well as calming the tension created from suppressing the emotions. It also creates a yin/yang balance throughout the whole system, giving the complexion a healthy glow.

End of the Day

Now we are coming to the end of the day and we do not wish to take our workday home. We want to leave it all behind and relax at home with the family.

Daily Healing Technique #16

Squeeze the small intestine at Si 1 (at the end of the little finger on the outside edge of the fingernail at the base, 1 fen to the side) to clear excessive heat from the heart, thus lessening the day's activity. This also increases the rate at which substances leave our bodies via the skin, so it takes out the junk that we have put in during the day, strengthens the body's defenses, and provides moisture and nourishment to the skin.

Squeezing Si 2 (in the hollow on the outside of the little finger before the second knuckle) dispels heat from the heart. It also promotes the circulation of substances to the kidney from the small intestine, aiding the kidney's control over fire and making the liver more yin (for reducing anger). This is a water point and has a cooling effect upon the body in general.

Daily Healing Technique #17

Do not press Si 3, just over that last knuckle, as this will cause the fire to burn!

Daily Healing Technique #18

K 1 (the only point on the bottom the foot) harmonizes the fire and water and has a balancing effect upon the whole body. It is a major revival point, as it releases qi from the kidneys, so it is a good point to use when you arrive home and are just too tired to play with the kids or pay attention to what your wife (or husband) has been up to (and aren't they the most important?).

Daily Healing Technique #19

Pressing straight in at K 2 (just in the hollow on the outside of the foot about 5 fen up from the ground) eliminates fire and cools the blood. It also balances the whole system with yin and yang qi.

Daily Healing Technique #20

Pressing K 10 (at the back of the knee and just to the right of the big tendon in the center for the right leg and vice versa) tonifies the kidneys and dispels heat, as well as regulating and soothing the lower heater.

So, you're going to bed now and need the lower heater to be soothed so that you are able to get a good night's sleep, which brings you back to the next day.

The Heart Starter (Diagrams 20-22)

As we have referred throughout this book to the human phenomenon of cardiac arrest due to the effect of many of the point strikes on the carotid sinus, I will include a way to start the heart other than CPR.

Get in back of the person and sit him up. Apply pressure to the St 11 points, located just above the collar bone notch where it is closest to the neck. This point, by the way, will also cause a person to feel really ill when it is struck even lightly or when great pressure is placed upon it straight downward. This is due to its action on the vagus nerve, which is directly connected to the heart and has a great effect upon it. The thumb pressure causes the vagus nerve

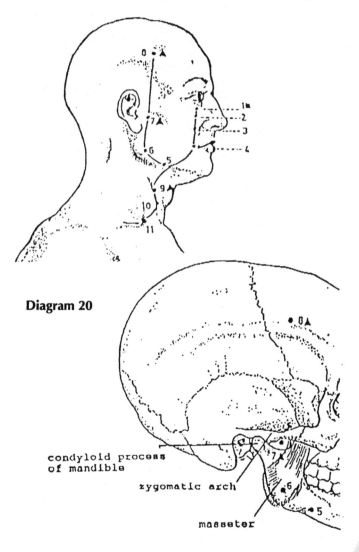

Diagram 20

condyloid process
of mandible

zygomatic arch

masseter

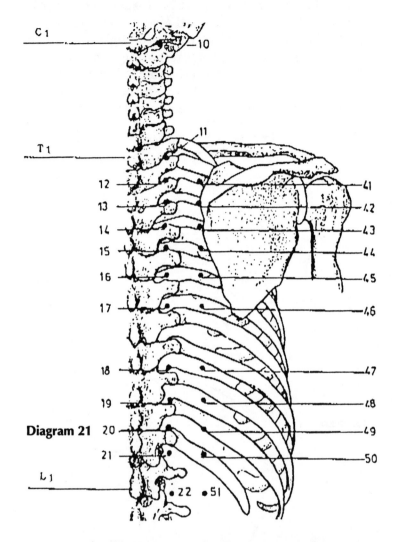

to activate the heart and helps in starting it. As soon as you have done this, you should strike to Bl 14 and 15 (on both sides of the backbone, five vertebra down from that large vertebra at the base of the neck) with a slipping, arcing motion on either side over the heart (using the flat of the palm). If this fails, then CPR is your only option.

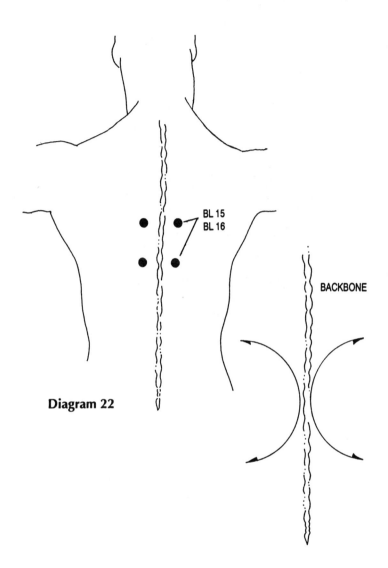

BL 15
BL 16

BACKBONE

Diagram 22

Dao Yin Exercises for
Converting the Sexual Energy for Use

Lie on the floor or in bed with your tongue on the hard palate. Breathe in as you raise your feet as high as you can. Drop the tongue to the lower palate as you breathe out and raise your bum as high as you can without allowing your shoulders to leave the bed (this is the time for your spouse to do nasty things to you!). The hands should be flat on the ground, palms down beside you.

Bring the tongue up again and breathe in as you lower the bum. Now as you breathe out, drop the tongue and bring your legs up to your chest and hug your shins tightly as you still breathe out. Hold it until you wish to breathe in again. Breathe in as you lower your legs, holding them at an angle of about 20 degrees for a few seconds and then lowering them to the floor.

Bring the tongue back up and breathe in again. Repeat this three times.

Chang Yiu-chun on Healing

Chang Yiu-chun was my main teacher in both the death arts and the healing arts. His knowledge was immense. What you are about to read comes from some of the hundreds of handwritten notes that I took during my brief training period with Chang Yiu-chun

Much of this has not been published because at times Master Chang becomes very confusing. (Actually, I believe that he is *trying* to confuse!) When I knew him, his sense of humor was greatly advanced but he was not trying to be funny, and some of this comes out in what follows.

> **E.M.:** I am interested in the fighting part of t'ai chi ch'uan. Are you able to elaborate on your previous statements?
> **C:** I have already stated that there is only one part of t'ai chi ch'uan as far as I am concerned and that the other part, the health, comes by itself. One does not begin t'ai chi ch'uan initially for good health. To do so, one is missing out on one very important aspect of one's training, and that is that the mind must be strong.

One of the ways that we maintain a strong mind is that we learn the wushu (fighting arts). In this way we are no longer afraid and our mind becomes more yang. Only then are we able to heal ourselves using t'ai chi ch'uan. What was it you asked?

E.M.: About the fighting.
C: Yes, t'ai chi ch'uan is a fighting art, but if we attempt to learn it in the same way that many of the other wushu styles are learned, then we fail.

E.M.: Is this because t'ai chi ch'uan is a soft style?
C: There are no soft fighting styles! How can there be? If you must fight someone, then you must in some way hurt them in order to defend yourself. T'ai chi ch'uan is not a soft style of fighting, and I have permanent injuries to prove this. No, the difference is that we must not be encumbered by set patterns of movement so that our mind must move in an unnatural way.

E.M.: But surely all of the movements that we learn in t'ai chi ch'uan are not so natural.
C: No, any movement that has to be taught is not a natural movement. However, there are certain movements that when they are learned are able to teach the body about spontaneous movement and replace our natural movement with more useful movement. The movements of t'ai chi ch'uan are like this. It takes some people 10 or 12 years before the unnatural movements of t'ai chi

ch'uan begin to teach them about their own body movement so that they are able to react with great speed and power to any attack from outside. Until that time, t'ai chi ch'uan is used in much the same way that other wushu is used.

E.M.: So after some time, something happens to change the t'ai chi ch'uan.

C: Yes, exactly. Our mind becomes like certain animals and we begin to regain certain animal instincts, those which we have lost over many centuries. Because our mind is now reunited with our bodies because of our t'ai chi ch'uan training, so too our body becomes more with animal instinct.

E.M.: Is this why we read and are taught so often to "have the eye of the eagle" or the "body of the monkey"?

C: I should not take this aspect too far as some of the wushu has done.

E.M.: What do you mean?

C: Some people have learned that we must act like animals, but this is incorrect. Physically, we cannot be like an animal; this is obvious, although I have seen some people who could be mistaken for some animals. What the classics say is that we must adopt the ways of thinking of the animals. This is very difficult for me to explain. Animals, for the most part, do not think, they just react using reactions that are like breathing is to us—it is automatic. And sometimes the animals are able to react even before the event has happened. This is because of the greater awareness built into all animals. When the human beings were tried out, we began to use our physical capabilities for thinking and that is where we lost much of our earlier instincts.

E.M.: Could I please interrupt here master Chang and ask you what you meant by humans were "tried out"?

C: That is another complete story that would take up many pages and wear out many of your pencils. There are some areas of taoist philosophy that cannot be written down in any book, and this is the part that has been lost. We are able to regain this part through the practice of t'ai chi ch'uan.

E.M.: You were talking about the animals.

C: Yes. Once we have done all of the training and we already know how to fight using the movements of t'ai chi ch'uan, then the ch'i (internal) part of t'ai chi ch'uan teaches us about the unknown.

E.M.: What is this unknown?

C: I am sorry, I do not know it!

E.M.: But what you did to me earlier, was that the unknown?

C: I do not know what I did to you earlier.

E.M.: You helped me up and put a wad onto my face, did you not?

C: Yes, I remember helping you, but I do not remember doing it to you, did you do something stupid?

E.M.: Yes, I ran at you, remember?

C: You should not run.

E.M.: I am a little confused now, please continue about the animals.
C: I once had some animals.

E.M.: Yes?
C: They started out as friends but after some years they became my teachers.

E.M.: What do you mean?
C: I began to notice that the birds, in particular, were looking at me wherever I was located but they never seemed to look in the same way that we look. The birds were looking at me, and every time I moved they would move accordingly, even if I moved behind them. This is when I discovered about the way of the internal mind and the parts of our inheritance that we have lost. I discovered that the animals are able to look not at our physical body but at the space surrounding that body and, in doing this, they are able to know exactly when we will move and when to move themselves without thinking about it.

E.M.: I am beginning to think that there is no real reason to actually learn the t'ai chi ch'uan forms as fighting applications.
C: Yes, there is a reason, and that is that we must be able to protect ourselves using our physical capabilities, and it is not many who will ever be able to rise to the highest levels. We do learn about the applications, but only to help us in our training. As I think I said before, if you learn each of the movements and try to use them in fighting, then you will be

defeated. We must react as the animals to whatever is happening to us.

E.M.: Does the pushing hands help in this aspect?

C: The pushing hands is a new invention, but it does help. It must be practiced for years and years against many different people in order that we learn about no mind movement [rough translation]. I have seen some people practicing pushing hands, and they like to pretend that they are fighting each other and trying to see who is better at it. This is like trying to see who is the better artist by trying to have some competition to see who is better at holding the brush!

I believe that the pushing hands is there only as a training help. When I was learning about t'ai chi ch'uan, we only had methods of training [rough translation]. These methods were more complete than today's pushing hands, but people need something definite to practice, and the pushing hands filled that need.

E.M.: I know about your ideas on pushing hands and that it should never be used for competition, but surely we must attack our opponent in order to learn.

C: We must attack in order to help ourselves. We learn to only attack at the opportune moment in time and body movement. If we attack at the wrong time, then the opponent will be ready for us and so we will be defeated. If we attack when the opponent is at his weakest, then we will win. This is what can be gained from the practice of pushing hands.

What I have said earlier is that the pushing hands should not become like fighting, where one man is trying to defeat another. If we have this thought in our minds then we will never be able to rise to the highest level of fighting because we are trying to defeat another human being, and that is not real human nature.

We do not wish to fight! We only fight because we are threatened physically, and then it should be to the death. In pushing hands we do not practice deadly techniques, only pulling and pushing. This teaches us about body movement and learning to move with another person. But there is also another area of pushing hands that can be detrimental to our t'ai chi ch'uan learning.

Until we have advanced our minds to a high level of fighting, we must move with the other person, and that usually means that when he comes forward in pushing hands, we move backward; the nature of the exercise dictates this. But this is not in keeping with the classics, which say that if he moves forward, so too do you move forward, and if he moves backward, so too do you move backward. So it is my view that when we do the pushing hands, even though we must move backward when he comes forward just to keep the movements smooth, our minds must be thinking the correct movements.

Conclusion

Many will buy this book for all the wrong reasons, but hopefully some of the nicer stuff will rub off and help these people achieve an inner balance.

Learn to laugh at yourself; the martial arts are not serious. We do not wear fancy dress, we just *do* the martial arts. You do not have to put on a special uniform; you can join the army to do that. The martial arts are flowing and beautiful, and so we just do them no matter what we are wearing.

Someone once asked me how he should prepare himself to do his training each day. I told him he should not prepare; his training should be a part of his everyday life and not something extra that he does. You could be putting out the washing and all of a sudden go into your forms practice, then go back to the washing without even thinking about it.

It's this way with my children, whom we home-school. We have made their education just learning, not schooling! Learning is a part of what they do, not something that they *must* do—nothing special. So now we have a 9-year-old boy who is giving piano concerts, but not because he "*has to* learn piano." Rather, the piano is just something he *does*. It's the same with his martial arts (and this is a very good reason not to send him to school!) In fact, all of our children simply do their training when they feel the need to; it's just something that everyone does.

It's amazing when I think about how difficult it was for me to learn the techniques because I began later in life (18 years old). Now my children just see a technique once and then they do it! Then when they do it again, they are doing it better than me.

One saying from the old Chinese texts that I have kept as being the most important in the martial arts is: "Don't live for your martial art, but rather, martial art to live."

Healing
Applications

This section deals with the t'ai chi healing and what it means. It's not just a matter of doing the form and hoping for the best! And it is also not a matter of just doing the postures and knowing what each is meant for. There are also secondary postures to use along with the major postures when the opposite condition applies. For instance, the main posture that treats the heart is regarded as being "yin." (Each organ is regarded as being either relatively yin or relatively yang, and its associated posture also takes on this attitude.) So we would use this posture by itself to treat only a "yang" disease state of the heart, such as too much sexual urge or premature ejaculation, etc. Because this posture is a yin posture, we would not use it alone to treat a yin disease state of the heart, such as low libido, no fire, or too laid back. We would have to add its partner posture, the one associated with the small intestine, which is yang in nature. So we would treat a yin disease state of the heart with two taiji postures and a yang disease state with only one posture.

ORGAN	POSTURES	STATE	CONDITION
COLON	Use Grasp Bird'sTail up to push. Repeat 10 times.	Yang	For a yin disease such as diarrhea, use this Qigong only.
	Use the Qigong for the lungs, i.e., Fishes in Eight. Go into it 10 times and hold as Qigong for one minute.	Yin	Use this as well as the above if the state is yang, such as constipation.
LUNGS	Fishes in Eight.	Yang	Use by itself if a yang condition, like inflammation, etc. But O.K. for all lung ailments.
	Grasp Bird's Tail as above.	Yang	Use if liquid on the lungs, etc., along w/Fishes in Eight or as an adjunct to it.
SPLEEN	High Pat on Horse. Use as static Qigong, holding five minutes on each side. Or use Horse's Mane as moving Qigong.	Yin	Use if too much yang in spleen.
LUNGS/ COLON	Pulling the Bow, plus Lift Hands to Heaven (that whole section that involves those two). Repeat five times.	—	Use is overall toning needed in both these areas.
LUNGS/ SPLEEN	In general, use Stroking the Horse's Mane. Be sure to swivel on heels. Repeat five times, holding for three minutes.	—	Use when spleen or lungs are malfunctioning. A general toner for these organs.

ORGAN	POSTURES	STATE	CONDITION
STOMACH	Tan Pien (Single Whip). Use as static Qigong to aid digestion. Or Wave Hands Like Clouds to balance out the energy.	Yang	Use Tan Pien for all stomach ailments or if too little stomach activity, i.e., too yin. Use Wave Hands to balance chi.
	Golden Cock Stands on One Leg. Use as static Qigong for three minutes on each leg.	—	Overall stomach problems.
	Hold Brush Knee Twist Step (BKTS) as static Qigong on each side for five minutes. Repeat three times.	—	Same as above.
	Play Guitar. Go into this from BKTS. Hold five minutes and repeat five times.	—	Aids in digestion.
	Wave Hands Like Clouds.	Yang	Use if not enough stomach activity. Good Qigong for stomach overall.
	Horse's Mane, use w/Wave Hands.	Yin	Use if too yang in stomach.
	Perform from push to apparent close-up and hold at end for one minute. Repeat 10 times.	—	Use for general gastric troubles.
	Wave Hands Like Clouds. Generally repeat 10 x 4 steps, but do as many as you like.	—	Same as above.
SPLEEN	Wave Hands Like Clouds.	Yin	Use w/the main one of Tan Pien if stomach acivity too yang, i.e., heartburn, etc.

ORGAN	POSTURES	STATE	CONDITION
SPLEEN/ STOMACH	Wave Hands Like Clouds.	Yang	Use w/the above if too little spleen activity, i.e., too yin.
LIVER	Step Back and Repulse Monkey.	Yang	Use w/the above if a yin condition exists, e.g., dull and listless, etc.
GALL BLADDER/ LIVER	Step Back and Repulse Monkey, Yang Cheng-fu.	Yang	If too yin, not enough bile, etc., or gall bladder is not working well. If bad lower back pain, especially in mornings, repeat five times, but also use for overall gall bladder.
	Lift Hands from Flying into It and hold for five minutes. on both sides.	Yin	Use if too much bile or activity too yang. Use w/the above.
	Lift Hands as static Qigong.	Yin	Use by itself for all liver ailments, but in particular if too angry (red face, etc.), i.e., too yang.
HEART	Brush Knee Twist Step. Moving Qigong.	Yin	Use for all heart states, but in particular if too much fire in heart, can't sleep, etc. Also for pre-ejaculation.
SMALL INTESTINE	Fan through Back. Hold the static Qigong for five minutes.	Yang	Use by itself for general small intestine conditions, but in particular if too little activity in small intestine, i.e., too yin.
SMALL INTESTINE/ HEART	Fan through Back	Yang	Use if too much sleep, not enough sexual urge, etc.

ORGAN	POSTURES	STATE	CONDITION
SMALL INTESTINE/ HEART	Brush Knee Twist Step.	Yin	Use w/Fan through back if too much small intestine activity, i.e., too yang.
KIDNEYS	Spin Around and Kick, Yang Cheng-fu style.	Yin	Use if too fearful.
	Snake Creeps Down. Repeat and hold three times on each side for three minutes if possible, less if not.	—	Use if kidneys need toning in general.
BLADDER	Mailed Fist and tan-tien pushing, from old Yang, plus bit from end when fist comes over face and around, bending backwards, etc.	Yang	Use for great sorrow.
	Spin Around and Kick. Use w/the above.	Yin	Unbalanced emotions.
KIDNEYS/ BLADDER	(Use w/the above.) Mailed Fist, old Yang, as well as tan-tien pushing and bit from end as above.	Yang	Use if too fearful.
TRIPLE WARMER	In general, start w/Three Warmer Qigong exercise.	—	This organ, generally not known about in Western medicine, is used for irregularity in other organs and if amount of yin and yang energy is unbalanced.
GATE OF LIFE ORGAN	Use the Opening of the Gates for this one.	—	Use for too little semen production in males and menstrual problems in females. Use if regenerative energy is irregular or if person is depressed. Again, this organ is generally unknown in the West.

ORGAN/AREA	POSTURES	STATE	CONDITION
ALL OF THE INTERNAL ORGANS	Go into Embrace Tiger, Return to Mountains from Cross Hands. Repeat 10 times.	—	Use if organs are in need of rejuvenation in general.
CNS	Shoulder Press. Go into it from Pull Back and hold for five minutes, then go into Stork Spreads Wings and hold for five minutes.	—	Acts upon the cerebrum, making it more alert. Good for exams, etc.
SPINAL COLUMN	Use Lift Hands as moving and static Qigong.	—	Use to make spinal column more elastic. Also for dry or wrinkled skin, to maintain more youthful appearance.
GLANDS	Step Forward, Parry, and Punch, from BKTS to punch. Hold at end for three minutes, repeat five times.	—	Use if glands are not functionng optimally.
JOINTS	Move into Tan Pien from Fishes in Eight and hold for three minutes on each leg.	—	Use for joint ailments.
BLOOD CIRC.	General Step Forward to Seven Stars. Hold as static Qigong for three minutes on each leg. Repeat three times.	—	Use for bad circulation.

ORGAN/AREA	POSTURES	STATE	CONDITION
—	From old Yang style use Fist under Elbow as many times as you like. Also use Lotus Kick.	—	Use if overweight.
—	Turn around and Chop with Fist, Yang Cheng-fu style.	—	Use if overweight.
—	Use Fist under Elbow from Yang Cheng-fu form and hold as Qigong for five minutes each side.	—	Use if underweight.
—	Needle at Sea Bottom. Go into this one from BKTS, hold for one minute, then slowly come up and repeat on other side.	—	Use to increase the life force to the spine, especially when used w/Lotus Kick, Yang Chen-fu style.
—	Separation of Right and Left Foot, Yang Cheng-fu style.	Yin	Use if person is too yang, angry, red in face, etc.
—	Separation of Left and Right Foot, old Yang style.	Yang	Use if person is too yin, too laid back. Lack of energy.
—	Sitting Like a Duck posture. Go into it from standing if possible. Hold for three minutes on each side. No good for older people who are arthritic, etc.	—	Body in need of rejuvenation.

YIN ORGANS	YANG ORGANS	IMPLICATIONS
These yin organs store energy for use later.	These yang organs activate energy, i.e., cause storage organs to release it to perform some function.	An imbalance of yin or yang energy in these main organs causes disease, so we try to balance the yin and yang energy using the above postures as Qigongs.
Liver Heart Spleen Lungs Kidneys	Gall Bladder Small Intestine Stomach Large Intestine/Colon Bladder	

Martial
Applications

In the following section I
have tried to present the major points used in this
book, their locations, a relatively easy application,
the result of such a strike, and the antidote where
applicable. All of the following is presented in greater
detail in the main text of this book. This is meant to
be used as a quick-reference guide to the points.

POINT	LOCATION	ACTIVATION
Gb 14	Above middle of the eyebrow, on forehead, 1 cun up.	Downward palm heel. Made more potent by strike/slide of other palm up on outside of arm or down on inside.
		Upward palm heel. Made more potent by strike down on outside of arm or up on inside of arm.
		Straight in.
Gb 1	By outside corner of eye.	Strike w/fingertips from back to front. Couple w/ strike/slide on arm against chi flow.
Gb 3	Temple.	Hard, straight in. Use a roundhouse punch if facing the person.
Gb 24	In 7th intercostal space, one rib below Liv 14.	Straight in.
Gb 24 + Liv 14	Under nipple in 6th intercostal space.	Straight in. Double palm heel, right fingers up and left fingers down, to hit on right side of person.
Gb 31	Lateral side of leg, where end of longest finger would hang.	Kick (roundhouse). More potent if wrist is grabbed—squeeze and twist to activate lung and heart meridians.

Note: The first line of defense for revival against a carotid sinus KO is Gb 20s, squeezing in and up. A carotid sinus KO can basically come from any Gb points.

POINT	LOCATION	ACTIVATION
Cv 22	Pit of neck.	Straight in, fingertip or chop.
Cv 22 + Gb 1	—	Fingertip back to front, then chop straight in.
Cv 21	Top of head (soft spot on babies).	Hit straight in (down). May need to hit in ribs first to bend him over, then strike Cv 21.

RESULT(S)	ANTIDOTE(S)
Drains energy from lower body. May not be able to get up. Maybe a KO.	1. Gb 20s, push up. 2. Gb 21s, push down (w/fingertips).
Rush of energy to top of body, especially brain. Dizziness, tongue out, convulsions. Possible KO.	1. Gb 20s, push down. 2. Gb 21s, push down (knife hand); pull away fast, down shoulder. 3. Si 4, push straight in, medium pressure. 4. CPR.
Not as potent as the other two, but KO is possible, also broken neck. Disorientation, swelling of tongue.	1. Gb 14, pull down. 2. Gb 21s, slap down. 3. CPR if heart has stopped.
Extreme nausea, loss of memory, possible death. Very dangerous, even w/light strike.	1. Rub Gb 1 backwards toward ear. 2. Gv 26 (under nose) press up and back toward head. Note: CPR not good w/o antidotes.
KO. Possible death. Small artery there can cause bleeding into brain w/ death three days later.	No revival points. Use CPR.
Knockout.	Gb 20s, straight in toward front of head.
Instant death.	No antidote if struck hard.
Paralyzes legs. Can be a KO, as for all Gb points.	Squeeze hit point in and then rub down the leg. If a KO, squeeze in and up on Gb 20s.
Death by crushing of trachea (suffocation).	No antidote points. Try CPR. Stretch anus sphincter (speeds up breathing).
Death.	No antidote points. Try CPR.
Power leaves lower body. Legs go. Heavy hit can cause death.	Li 10. Press in fairly hard if legs are just weak. (Brings chi back.)

POINT	LOCATION	ACTIVATION
Gv 26	Under nose.	Upward strike.
Mind Point	Where fat is in front of jaw angle.	Hit in (roundhouse punch) toward back of head.
		Strike straight in.
Cv 24	In chin indentation.	Receiver's left to right. Use fingertips. Also slap/rub down on inside of attacker's right arm.
		Receiver's right to left, and slap/slide up on outside of attacking arm. Can also be struck straight in.
St 9	One of the main points along the carotid artery.	Straight back in toward back of head. Fingertips are best, but fist, shuto, knife edge of palm, etc., are possible. Can be combined w/P 6 in a distal direction.

Note: Doctors occasionally use St 9 to lower blood pressure and heart activity. Press Gb 20s in and up, for intestine and groin strikes as well as GB attacks.

POINT	LOCATION	ACTIVATION
Cv 17	Centerline of chest between nipples.	Palm striking downward. Combine w/ descending strike (back of hand) on inside of arm.
		Palm striking upward.

Note: When P 6 is struck, it causes chi to rush there, leaving other points more vulnerable.

POINT	LOCATION	ACTIVATION
Cv 14	Below sternum, between K 21s.	Strike straight in (palm heel, etc.). Heart mu point (i.e., directly associated w/ heart and can stop it.)
		Strike downward (palm heel, elbow, knuckles, etc.).
		Strike upward. Doesn't take much if person is already angry; blood pressure is high.

RESULT(S)	ANTIDOTE(S)
Could cause death. Most nerves in body just give up.	1. For KO, put palm on top of Gv 21, push downward lightly. 2. Extra point: fish's belly, middle of eyebrow. Push in and slightly downward.
Cuts off signals from CNS to brain.	Rub backward (opposite of strike direction) on point; also Gb 20s, push straight in.
KO or death, depending on power of strike.	Rub Gb 3s (right hand ccw, left cw); slap down on Gb 21s; repeat.
Extreme nausea, vomiting, KO.	Rub Cv 4 ccw (to person doing the rub).
Same as above.	Rub Cv 4 cw (to person doing the rub) and push in slightly.
KO. Tricks the body into thinking blood pressure is too high; heart slows (or stops), and pressure drops dramatically.	For KOs due to blood pressure drop, put person on back, elevate legs, then push up on Gb 20s. Make sure airway is open in case windpipe got hit.
Upsets diaphragm (seat of power). Power is drained from lower body.	Place thumb on Cv 17 and push up, breathing out. Brings chi back to diaphragm area.
Spasm in lower body; goes stiff, falls down.	Thumb on Cv 17, push down.
Death point. Can't even be needled in acupuncture. Probably most forbidden point in acupuncture.	None. Try CPR.
Drains lungs and heart of energy.	Elevate feet. Rub Cv 14 in cw direction. Try CPR.
"Chi topping" causes heart to over-react, creating extreme high blood pressure. KO.	Put on back and tweak St 9.

POINT	LOCATION	ACTIVATION
Liv 19	Corner of shoulder, anterior.	Finger strike, straight in. Combine w/ distally directed P 6 strike.
Liv 14	Below nipple. Intercostal space between 6th and 7th ribs, where pectoral muscle makes crease.	Strike left to right or right to left (knuckles, etc.). Can use w/P 6.
		Strike straight in.
Liv 13	Free end of tip of 11th rib.	Fist in a side strike, hooked fist. Stand at 90° to opponent and strike to his side.
Lu 3	Lateral side of biceps, just distal to deltoid.	Punch.
P 6, H 3, Liv 6, K 9	Lower leg.	Punch-kick retaliation to right-left punch attack. Strike down on P 6 and H 3.
Liv 8 + Cv 2	Crease of knee when leg is bent. Pubic bone.	Two-hand strike-block of roundhouse kick to hit Li 8, then slide into elbow Cv 2.
Lu 2	Happy point, just below outer end of clavicle.	Press straight in.
H 3	Inside crease of elbow. A major point on the body.	Usually struck in a distal direction. Thumb knuckle works well. Can combine w/upward slap on outside of arm.
		Struck proximally w/thumb knuckle, same direction, on inside of other arm, plus carotid sinus as third point.
		Strike straight in.

RESULT(S)	ANTIDOTE(S)
Paralyzes arm. Possible liver damage.	1. Liv 14, push in lightly. 2. Liv 3, push in lightly, and Li 3 (also good for knee problems). If liver is suspected, see an acupuncturist.
KO or blurred vision. Extreme liver problems. Person may even go blind over a certain period.	Massage Liv 14 in opposite direction of strike. Massage Liv 3 and Gv 20 (can just put palm on entire top of head to massage).
Problems w/mind (e.g., extreme anxiety, collapse); possible KO. Stops chi of whole body for a moment.	Massage in on Liv 14, or see an acupuncturist if mind problems are indicated.
Vomiting, diarrhea on the spot, lack of power in lower body, extreme emotional disturbances.	Liv 14, press in Liv 13 (right side), massage ccw. Lu 3, massage.
Lungs can go into spasm. Major point for "time" striking. (Lu 3 is activated at lung's special time of day.)	Squeeze tip of thumb while pressing in on L 9.
Extreme mind confusion.	K 1, K 5. Squeeze in on both sides of Achilles tendon.
Severe liver and genital or kidney damage (blood in urine).	K 1, 7-second press-in (almost to point of pain) while patient breathes in; 7-second release while patient breathes out. K-5 and Gb 23s, 24s, press in.
Helps relieve tension.	An antidote for strikes that cause mind problems.
Can stop heart. Makes "mind point" very vulnerable. A light follow-up strike here puts a person out very easily.	H 3, rub in opposite direction. H 9 (little finger) will help in any case where a a heart point has been struck, as squeezing it increases heart activity. CPR.
High blood pressure.	H 9. S 9, tweak a bit. CPR.
Will weaken heart over time; therefore called delayed death touch.	H 9 if person isn't hurt too bad. CPR.

POINT	LOCATION	ACTIVATION
H 1	Armpit.	Tips of fingers. Can be used in combination w/wrist points.

Note: Pressure-point antidotes work only if you haven't been hit really hard. For a person struck hard, do CPR and call the paramedics. Another way to start the heart: sit person up and, from behind him, press down onto notch of collar bone at St 11 w/thumbs on either side of neck. This activates vagus nerve, which will cause heart to start. Also, strike on left side of backbone w/heel of palm using a circular blow inward to B 1, 14, and 15 (over the heart).

POINT	LOCATION	ACTIVATION
H 5	1 cun up from wrist under ulna.	Strike distally w/back of hand, lower knuckles, etc. Can be pressed on in a wrist lock, in conjunction w/Tw 12 or just when pushing on a weak elbow.
H 5 + Lu 8	Almost across from each other on wrist.	Squeeze.
		Strike straight in.
		Pull distally.
Co 10	On outside of forearm, 1 cun back from elbow crease.	Strike in and upward.
		Strike downward.
		Strike straight in.
Co 12	On outside of upper arm in depression just above elbow crease.	Strike downward w/back of wrist.

LARGE INTESTINE #10 (handwritten)

LARGE INT #12 (handwritten)

Note: Co points are also good for frontal headaches.

POINT	LOCATION	ACTIVATION
P 6	Middle of forearm, about one hand's width back from wrist crease.	Strike straight in.
		Strike distally.
		Strike proximally.

RESULT(S)	ANTIDOTE(S)
Heart stops.	Only CPR.
Severe energy drain.	H 5, pull lightly in a distal way, then H 3 in a proximal way.
Causes chi to rush to this area, leaving other points more vulnerable. Any face strike will be more potent.	Massage H 5 and Lu 6 distally.
Causes body to drain chi.	Same as above.
Heart and lungs may quiver; body loses chi.	Same as above.
Lower body loses chi; nausea.	Li 1, squeeze (outside of index finger-nail). Also Li 4.
Bowels may open up.	Li 10, massage in same direction w/ medium pressure. Li 1, squeeze.
Lower abdomen goes into spasm; arm becomes paralyzed. May be residual diarrhea for a couple of days.	Use two knuckles to pull/massage distally, full length of forearm.
Energy drain; may fall down and not be able to continue.	Squeeze arm on point and pull down.
Drainage point. Affects heart. Nausea, lack of power in lower body.	Press in on point.
Heart misses a couple of beats; person can't go on. Yin-yang balance of whole body is upset.	Tw 5 and 6 (opposite side of arm), knock three times w knuckles, distally. May need to be repeated.
Mind scatters.	Rub point in same direction.

POINT	LOCATION	ACTIVATION
P 6 + St 9	—	Slam his right wrist point (P 6) w/left palm a split second before striking into St 9 w/knife edge of right palm.
P 6, Tw 8 Cv 24	(Tw 8 is on outside of forearm, about halfway up in middle.)	Hit in succession.
Tw 17	Just behind lower part of ear, posterior to lobe, in depression between the angle of the mandible and the mastoid process.	Strike from back to front, using shuto. Can be preceded by striking up on outside of arm.
Tw 8	On outside of forearm, about halfway up in middle.	Strike straight in.
Tw 12	In horseshoe of triceps.	Strike after P 6.
Bl 10	On either side of neck, just under occipital bone.	Rabbit chop on neck, straight in.
Bl 6	Top of head, just to side of midline.	Strike in a backward direction.
St 15, 16	Pectorals, 2nd intercostal space. Just under St 15, in a bit toward midline in 3rd intercostal space.	Strike downward w/palm heel.
		Strike upward.
		Twist palms. Right cw, left ccw (best). Demonstrate w/push twist, not hard blow.
St 15, 16, Gb 24	—	Left palm heel strikes straight in to Gb 24 while right palm strikes from left to right, ending up at St 16.
Lu 3	On biceps.	Punch straight in.

RESULT(S)	ANTIDOTE(S)
KO. Takes energy from body.	Gb 20s, squeeze upward.
Dangerous combination. Irreversible damage to heart and chi system. Can cause death years later.	None really. Years of acupuncture may help.
Death. Mind goes dead.	None, not even CPR.
Blood pressure goes up; person may faint.	St 9, tweak.
Arm paralyzed.	Shake arm, rub down on top of arm and forearm, then slap on top of forearm.
Takes energy from kidneys, possible kidney failure then death. Light strike causes light-headedness; heavier strike can cause emotional problems later.	K 1, massage. Bl channels, rub up from kidney area toward shoulders.
Light blow stops fight. Drains power from lower body.	Rub in opposite direction, toward front of head.
Heart could stop. Light strike could stop fight.	H 1 and 3, massage in. CPR if heart stopped.
Heart could stop from too much energy.	Same as above.
Energy drainage (lower body) system as well as heart stoppage.	Massage Cv 4 both cw and ccw (tan-tien point).
Instant death.	Only CPR.
Upsets balance of chi between head and body. Extreme vertigo, fear of heights, extreme sadness but inability to express it by crying, etc.	Press Lu 2 (happy point). Press Lu 3. In extreme cases, see an acupuncturist.

POINT	LOCATION	ACTIVATION
Cv 4	Tan tien (3 cun below midline on navel).	Upward strike (kick).
		Downward strike (fist or knee).
		Straight in.
Cv 6	Halfway between tan tien and navel.	Straight in. Large part of Cv meridian may be hit by a hinge blow (elbow on top, forearm vertical).
Cv 4 + Cv 14	Tan tien.	Double palm strike, one right above the other.
K 5 .	Near Achilles tendon.	Foot stomp, struck downward.
Mind Point + Gv 26	By jaw hinge.	Hit P 6 distally in block, then right backfist to mind point, then right elbow to Gv 26.
Sp 20 + Liv 14	—	Fingers of left hand to Sp 20, right palm to Liv 14. (Part of the 12 secret techniques.)

Note: St 9 also forms a bad combination w/Liv 14.

Sp 21 + St 9	On lat.	Left fingers to St 9, right wrist (arms crossed) to Sp 21.

RESULT(S)	ANTIDOTE(S)
Increases blood pressure, may cause fainting, possible death.	Tweak St 9.
Energy drain. Person falls down. Massage Cv 14 (heart shu point) lightly. Press Cv 1.	Press Gv 26 upward and backward.
Dangerous point. Causes energy to slow up, blackout, sickness. Could cause death.	Put person on side, leg drawn up. (coma position). Rub chest area down, push up under nose at Gv 26.
Potent strike. Hinge blow takes out a large part of Cv meridian.	Same as above.
Death if struck hard and simultaneously.	CPR if not struck too hard.
Dizziness, disorientation, possible blackout, blood in urine.	Press on K 5 and K 1.
Disrupts CNS, person falls to ground quivering. Nervous breakdowns later in life (if able to be resuscitated). Bad combination.	Shen men, or "Doorway to the Spirit." A calming rub proximally.
Whole body goes numb and paralyzed. Lungs and heart stop. Liv 14 is a death point by itself.	None.
KO and extreme spleen damage and failure. Lungs contract.	Sp 20 and 21, massage downward. Gb 20s, massage up.

About the Author

Erle Montaigue is one of the leading instructors of the internal arts of t'ai chi ch'uan, pa-kua chang, and qigong, and is recognized internationally as such.

He received the degree of master when he became the first Westerner to perform at the All China National Wushu Tournament in May of 1985 and is, we believe, the only Westerner to have received such an honor. Erle was tested for hours by three of the world's greatest masters in China. He has been practicing the internal arts since 1968 and is able to trace his lineage in a straight line back to the founder of the Yang style, Yang Lu-Ch'an. He was one of the first students of Chu King-Hung, who was one of first students of the late Yang Sau-Chung, the eldest son of Yang Cheng-Fu. Erle has had many other great teachers from China as well. He has taught in

London, and he is one of the only Westerners to have taught t'ai chi back to the Chinese in Hong Kong in 1981. He now teaches in Australia.

Erle is also one of the main students of Chang Yiu-Chun, the late student of Yang Shao-Hou. Chang taught Erle the secrets of the original Yang style (old Yang Lu-ch'an style and also the art of dim-mak), which actually is t'ai chi ch'uan.

Erle is the vice chairman of the Federation of Australian Wushu and Kung Fu Organizations and is the course coordinator of the T'ai Chi and Pa-Kua sections of the National Coaching Accreditation Scheme for kung fu. He is also the first t'ai chi person to be given Level Two of the Sports Accreditation Scheme for t'ai chi and pa-kua. This level is considered to be of Olympic standard, if t'ai chi (heaven forbid) were an Olympic sport! He is also president of the Australian Therapeutic Movement Association and head of the World Taiji Boxing Association. This association boasts schools in more than 23 countries, all of which have learned t'ai chi in some way from Erle Montaigue. Erle is also the editor of the international magazine called *Combat and Healing,* distributed worldwide.

Schools all around the world now use the Erle Montaigue name in their teaching. Erle has taught in Hong Kong, London, and Sydney, Australia, and has given workshops all around the world. Articles authored by Erle Montaigue have appeared in almost every international martial arts magazine, and his often provocative statements have helped to make t'ai chi and pa-kua the great fighting arts that they are known to be today.

His eight books are published worldwide, as are his 46 (as of 1992) self-teaching videos. People around the world have learned t'ai chi or pa-kua in this way, and they probably never would have been able to do so had it not been for these videos. Many of the world's leading karate teachers, as high as sixth dan, have learned from Erle's videos and attended his workshops.

Before t'ai chi kung-fu, Erle Montaigue was well versed in the Western art of amateur and professional wrestling, which he now brings into his classes as an adjunct to the kung-fu training. Erle is also an accomplished modern musician, having had albums recorded under his name.

He now travels to the United States, Canada, and Europe twice per year to teach martial arts, as well as leading workshops in New Zealand and Australia.

Erle Montaigue has, at the time of this printing, 46 video titles covering every possible aspect of the martial arts/healing arts, including taiji, dim-mak, bagwa, qigong, iron shirt qigong, weapons, and the Montaigue system. If you would like a free catalog of these titles, please write to:

MTG VIDEO
P.O. Box 792
Murwillumbah NSW 2484
Australia
Fax: (your overseas code) + 61-66-797028